JN086666

The Chemical History of a Candle

by Michael Faraday

Level 4
(2000-word)

Rewritten by Andrew Robbins

IBC パブリッシング

はじめに

　ラダーシリーズは、「はしご (ladder)」を使って一歩一歩上を目指すように、学習者の実力に合わせ、無理なくステップアップできるよう開発された英文リーダーのシリーズです。

　リーディング力をつけるためには、繰り返したくさん読むこと、いわゆる「多読」がもっとも効果的な学習法であると言われています。多読では、「1. 速く 2. 訳さず英語のまま 3. なるべく辞書を使わず」に読むことが大切です。スピードを計るなど、速く読むよう心がけましょう（たとえば TOEIC® テストの音声スピードはおよそ1分間に150語です）。そして1語ずつ訳すのではなく、英語を英語のまま理解するくせをつけるようにします。こうして読み続けるうちに語感がついてきて、だんだんと英語が理解できるようになるのです。まずは、ラダーシリーズの中からあなたのレベルに合った本を選び、少しずつ英文に慣れ親しんでください。たくさんの本を手にとるうちに、英文書がすらすら読めるようになってくるはずです。

《本シリーズの特徴》

• 中学校レベルから中級者レベルまで5段階に分かれています。自分に合ったレベルからスタートしてください。

• クラシックから現代文学、ノンフィクション、ビジネスと幅広いジャンルを扱っています。あなたの興味に合わせてタイトルを選べます。

• 巻末のワードリストで、いつでもどこでも単語の意味を確認できます。レベル1、2では、文中の全ての単語が、レベル3以上は中学校レベル外の単語が掲載されています。

• カバーにヘッドホーンマークのついているタイトルは、オーディオ・サポートがあります。ウェブから購入／ダウンロードし、リスニング教材としても併用できます。

《使用語彙について》

レベル1：中学校で学習する単語約1000語

レベル2：レベル1の単語＋使用頻度の高い単語約300語

レベル3：レベル1の単語＋使用頻度の高い単語約600語

レベル4：レベル1の単語＋使用頻度の高い単語約1000語

レベル5：語彙制限なし

Contents

【本書に出てくる主な化学用語等】

あ

亜鉛	zinc	青みをおびた銀白色の金属。硫酸などの酸と反応して水素を発生する。トタン板など鉄鋼製品のめっき、乾電池の負極、真ちゅうや洋銀などの合金に使われる
アルカリ	alkali	水に溶けて強い塩基性（酸と結合して塩を生成する性質）を示す物質
アンチモン	antimony	銀白色の金属光沢をもつ半金属元素。メッキ、活字合金、軸受合金、半導体、医薬品などに用いられる
一酸化二窒素	nitrous oxide	亜酸化窒素、笑気ガスとも言い、酸素に触れると化合して褐色の二酸化窒素となる
塩酸	muriatic acid	塩化水素の水溶液。胃液の主成分
塩素酸塩	chlorate	塩素酸の水素が金属元素で置換されて生じる塩
塩素酸カリウム	potassium chlorate	熱すると酸素を放って分解するので酸化剤に用いられる。硫黄、リン、有機物などと混ぜると加熱、衝撃などによって爆発。マッチ、花火など爆薬の原料、漂白剤、医薬品の製造に用いられる

か

化学親和力	chemical affinity	化合物をつくる際に元素間に働くと考えられる結びつきやすさ
カリウム	potassium	軟らかい銀白色の金属。化学的には非常に活性で、水、酸素、酸と激しく反応する。水と反応すると水素を発生し、水酸化カリウムを生成する
カルシウム	calcium	単体は銀白色の軟らかい金属。酸や温水とは激しく反応して水素を発生する。天然には大理石・石灰岩・石膏などに含まれる。骨、歯などの主成分
黒色火薬	gunpowder	硝石、木炭、硫黄の粉末を混ぜた火薬。火薬の中で最も古くから用いられ、今日では花火や口火などに使用

さ

酸化剤	oxidizer	酸化作用をもつ物質。酸素を与える物質、水素をうばう物質、電子を受け取る物質をいう。過マンガン酸カリウムなど
酸化物	oxide	酸素と他の元素との化合物
酸化マンガン	manganese oxide	黒褐色の粉末である二酸化マンガンは、高温に熱すると分解し酸素を発生する。酸化剤、染料、釉、マッチ、乾電池、マンガン鋼の材料として利用される

三硫化アンチモン	antimony trisulfide	灰色の光沢ある結晶性の塊状物質, あるいは灰黒色の粉末。濃塩酸と反応し硫化水素を発生する。輝安鉱として天然に産する。色ガラス, マッチ, 花火の製造に, また顔料として用いられる
三硫化物	trisulfide	複数の硫黄原子が直接結合した構造を持つ多硫化物の一つ。硫化物とは, 硫黄とそれよりも陽性の元素との化合物。多くは酸により分解して硫化水素を発生する
真ちゅう(製品)	brass	銅と亜鉛の合金
石松子	lycopodium	ヒカゲノカズラ(ヒカゲノカズラ科の常緑性シダ)の胞子から作った粉末。花粉増量剤として使われる
石灰	lime	生石灰(酸化カルシウム), または, 消石灰(水酸化カルシウム)のこと
石灰岩[石]	limestone	炭酸カルシウムを主成分とする堆積岩。海底に堆積した生物の遺骸が堆積した生物岩と, 化学的沈殿による化学岩とがある。建築用材や石灰, セメントの原料など広く用いられる

た

炭酸カルシウム	calcium carbonate	酸に溶けて二酸化炭素を発生し, 二酸化炭素を含む水には炭酸水素カルシウムとなって溶ける。天然には方解石, 石灰石, 大理石などとして産出。セメント, 顔料, 歯がき粉, 医薬品などに使用される
炭素	carbon	炭素族元素の一つ。無定形炭素・黒鉛・ダイヤモンドの三つの同素体が存在するが, 化合物としては岩石圏, 水圏, 大気圏, 生物圏などに非常に豊富に存在する。きわめて融解しにくく, 高温では昇華する
炭酸塩	carbonate	炭酸の水素原子が金属で置換されて生じる塩
窒素	nitrogen	単体は無色・無味・無臭の気体。空気中に体積で約78パーセント含まれる。室温では不活性で燃焼に関与しない。高温では多くの元素と直接反応する
抵抗	resistance	加えられた力に対して, それと反対の方向にはたらく力。特に, 物体や流水の運動をさまたげ, エネルギーの損失を伴う現象
テレピン(精)油	turpentine	松やにから得られる揮発性の精油。無色ないし淡黄色で特異臭のある液体。溶剤・ワニス・ペイントなどの製造, 油絵の材料などに使用
電気分解	electrolysis	電解質水溶液あるいは溶融塩などのイオン伝導体に, 電流を流して化学変化をおこさせること

な		
鉛	lead	青白色の軟らかくて重い金属。加工が容易。空気中では表面が酸化されて被膜となるが，内部に及ばない。鉛管・電線被覆材・はんだ・活字合金・蓄電池極板・放射線遮蔽材などに使用される
二酸化炭素	carbon dioxide	炭素とその化合物の完全燃焼，生物の呼吸や発酵の際などに生じる気体。無色，無臭，不燃性の気体で空気より重い
二酸化物	dioxide	酸素2原子が他の元素と結合した化合物
は		
パイント	pint	単位；英国で約0.568リットル
プラチナ	platinum	銀白色の貴金属。化学的にはきわめて安定で王水以外の酸に不溶。酸化・還元の触媒やるつぼ・電極・理化学用器械・装飾品などに用いる
平方インチ (in²)	square inch	$1\ in^2 = 6.45\ cm^2$
飽和溶液	saturated solution	一定温度のもとで溶解しうる最大の溶質を溶かした溶液
ボルタ電池	voltaic pile	1800年ごろにイタリアのボルタによって発明された，希硫酸の溶液に，銅を正極，亜鉛を負極として入れた電池
ポンド	pound	重量の単位。453.6g
ま		
マンガン	manganese	純粋な単体は銀白色。空気中では表面が酸化される。希酸に溶けて水素を発生させる。鉄鋼業において脱酸，脱硫剤，また合金の構成金属として広く用いられている
綿火薬	guncotton	火薬類に用いられるニトロセルロース。精製した綿花を硫酸と硝酸で処理して作る。無煙火薬とダイナマイトの原料となる
毛細管現象	capillary action	液体中に立てた毛管内の液面が，管外の液面より高く，または低くなる現象
ら		
立方インチ (in³)	cubic inch	$1\ in^3 = 16.36\ cm^3$
立方フィート (ft³)	cubic foot	$1\ ft^3 = 1,728\ in^3 = 28,317\ cm^3$
硫酸	sulfuric acid	工業上もっとも重要な強酸の一つ
リン	phosphorus	非金属元素の一つ。黄リン（白リン）・紫リン・黒リンなどの同素体がある。黄リンは蝋状の固体で毒性が強く，空気中に置くと自然発火する

Lecture I:
The Flame and
Its Sources

第1講　炎とその源

　この6回の講義では、ロウソクの化学史を説明します。自然科学を理解するのに、ロウソクを研究することほど適した方法はありません。まずはロウソクの炎とその源について説明します。さて、ロウソクは、固形物なのにどうして炎が上がるのでしょうか。

【第1講に出てくる主な用語や表現】

ページ

3	vessel	器,（体内の）管
	wick	（ろうそくなどの）芯
	solid substance	固体
	fluid	液体
	current	流れ
4	gravity	重力, 引力
	guttering	ろうそくの溶けたろうが流れること
	irregularity	不規則
	ascending current	上昇気流
5	gutter	溶けたろうそくのろうの流出
	combustion	燃焼
	combustible	可燃の, 可燃性の
6	capillary action	毛細管現象
	porous	多孔質の
	saturated solution	飽和溶液
	solution	溶液
7	vaporous	蒸気質の
8	vapor	蒸気
	taper	細長い小ろうそく
	condensed	凝縮された
10	multitude	多数

In these six lectures, I will explain to you the chemical history of a candle. There is no better way to understand the natural sciences than by studying a candle. Therefore, I think you will not be disappointed with this subject.

Let us start with the light of the candle, which is different from the light of a lamp. With a lamp, you pour oil into a **vessel**, put in some moss or cotton, and then light the top of the **wick**. When the flame runs down the cotton to the oil, it gets extinguished, but it continues burning in the part above. However, with a candle, you have a **solid substance** with no vessel to contain it. This substance is not a **fluid**. How can it rise up to the flame? And when it becomes a fluid, how does it stay together?

When the candle burns, a beautiful cup is formed at the top. The heat of the candle draws up a **current** of air. This air cools the outside of the candle, keeping it solid, while the wax inside gets melted by the flame. The flame runs down the wick as far as it can go before it is extinguished. If the current of air went up only one side, the cup would be uneven and the fluid would run over the side. The same force of **gravity** that holds the world together also holds this fluid in a horizontal position. If the cup were not horizontal, the fluid would run away in **guttering**. Therefore, you see that the cup is formed by this steady rising current of air on all sides, which keeps the exterior of the candle cool.

A fuel that does not give rise to a cup would not make a good candle. Here I have some other beautiful candles with irregular shapes. If you burned them, they would not be able to form a proper cup's edge. I hope you will now see that the perfection of a process is itself beautiful. It is not the best-looking thing that is the most advantageous to us. Instead, it is the best acting thing. This good-looking candle is a bad-burning one. There will be a guttering because of the **irregularity** of the stream of air and the imperfection of the cup that forms.

You may see some pretty examples of the action of the **ascending current** when you have a little

gutter run down the side of a candle, making it thicker there than it is elsewhere. As the candle goes on burning, the gutter stays in place and forms a little pillar sticking up by the side. This is because it rises higher above the rest of the wax, and the air gets better around it, so it is more cooled. The cooler wax is more able to resist the action of the heat at a little distance. Now, the greatest mistakes and faults with regard to candles, as in many other things, often teach us important lessons. We have all come here to be scientists, and I hope you will always remember that whenever we see a result, especially if it's a new one, we should say, "What is the cause? Why does it occur?" In time, you will find out the reason.

Now, let us consider how the fluid gets out of the cup, up the wick, and into the flame, where **combustion** takes place. You already know that the flames on these burning wicks do not run down to the wax and melt it all away. They are separated from the fluid below and do not directly affect the sides of the cup. A **combustible** thing like that, which gradually burns away and is never consumed by the flame, is a very beautiful sight. It is especially beautiful when you consider the power of the flame to destroy the wax when it draws too near.

But how does the flame get hold of the wax? It is **capillary action** that moves the fuel to the part where combustion goes on. Now, I am going to give you two examples of capillary action. It is that kind of action or attraction that makes two things that do not dissolve in each other still hold together. When you wash your hands, you wipe off the water with a towel. Just as the towel becomes wet with water, it is that kind of attraction that makes the wick wet with wax. If you throw the towel over the side of the basin, it will draw the water out just the same.

Take a look at this. I have a column of salt, which is rather **porous**. Into the plate at the bottom, I will pour a **saturated solution** of salt that cannot absorb more [Fig. 1]. I have added a blue dye to the fluid so you can see it better. We can consider the plate to be the candle, the salt to be the wick, and the solution to be the melted wax. Observe that as I pour the fluid, it gradually rises up the column to the top.

If the blue solution were combustible and there were a wick at the top of the column, the solution

[Fig. 1] A plate with a column of salt in a saturated solution of salt shows the same capillary action that occurs in a candle.

would burn as it entered the wick.

Why doesn't the candle burn all the way down the wick? It is because the melted wax extinguishes the flame. If you turn a candle upside down so that the fuel can run down the wick, the candle will be extinguished. The reason is that the flame has not had time to make the fuel hot enough to burn. When the candle is right side up, only small quantities of wax are pulled into the wick.

In order to understand the **vaporous** condition of the fuel, I will show you a pretty experiment. If you blow a candle out carefully, you will see the

vapor rise from it like this [Fig. 2]. Now, if I hold a lighted **taper** a few inches from the wick, you will observe a train of fire going through the air until it reaches the candle. I must be quick because if I allow the vapor time to cool, it will become **condensed** into a liquid or solid, or the stream of combustible matter will get disturbed.

Now, onto the shape and form of the flame. It's important to know about the condition the matter of the candle finally assumes at the top of the wick.

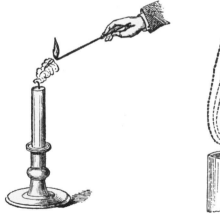 

[Fig. 2] A candle is relit by putting a flame to the vapor just after the candle is blown out.

[Fig. 3] The candle's flame is brighter at the top than at the bottom.

The form of the flame changes according to the size of the candle and atmospheric disturbances. It is a bright oblong that is brighter at the top than at the bottom [Fig. 3]. Besides the wick in the middle, there are certain darker parts toward the bottom, where the ignition is not as perfect as the part above.

In this drawing I have here, you can see how the surrounding atmosphere is essential to the flame [Fig. 4]. There is a current formed, which draws the flame out. You can see this by taking a lighted candle and putting it in the sun to cast its shadow on a piece of paper. How remarkable it is that that thing, which is light enough to produce shadows of other objects, can be made to throw its own shadow on a piece of white paper.

You observe the shadow of the candle and of the wick. Then there is a darkish part and then

[Fig. 4] The atmosphere surrounding a candle draws the flame out.

9

a part that is more distinct. Curiously, however, what we see in the shadow as the darkest part of the flame is actually the brightest part. Here you see the ascending current of hot air streaming upwards, drawing out the flame, supplying it with air, and cooling the sides of the cup of melted fuel.

There are a few additional points I would like to make. First, many of the flames you see here vary in their shape because of the currents of air blowing around them in different directions. By taking photographs of them, we can learn more about them. Second, if we have a flame sufficiently large, we can see it does not keep such a uniform shape. Instead, it breaks out with a power of life that is quite wonderful. You can see those fine tongues of flame rising up. But the general structure of the flame is the same as that of a candle. Why is this? Because, through the force of the current and the irregularity of the action of the flame, it cannot flow in one uniform stream. The air flows in so irregularly that the flame is broken up into a variety of forms, and each of these little tongues has an independent existence of its own. Indeed, you could say you have here a **multitude** of independent candles.

You must not imagine that the flame is of this particular shape just because you see these tongues all at once. They do not occur all at once. It is only because we see these shapes in such rapid succession that they seem to us to exist all at one time [Fig. 5].

Here we must stop, for our time is at its limit. Let us continue to look at the science behind the candle in the next lecture.

[Fig. 5] When each individual moment of a flame is examined as a photograph, different forms can be observed.

Lecture II:
The Brightness of
the Flame

第2講　炎の輝き

　前回の講義では、ロウソクの液体部分について説明しました。ちゃんと燃えたロウソクは、燭台に汚れを残すことなく完全に消えてしまいます。今回は、炎の部分によって何が起こるのか、そしてロウソクはどこへ行くのか、に焦点を当てます。

【第2講に出てくる主な用語や表現】

In the last lecture, we discussed the fluid portion of a candle. Today, we will focus on what happens in different parts of the flame, why it happens, what it does, and where the candle goes. After all, a candle that burns properly disappears completely without leaving any dirt in the candlestick. Curious, isn't it? We will examine the dark part of the flame first.

If I take this bent glass tube and place one end into the dark part of the flame [Fig. 6], immediately you can see that something is coming from the flame. At the other end of the tube, I have put a **flask**. You can see that something from the middle part of the flame is gradually drawn out through the tube and into the flask. It behaves differently from how it does in the open air. It not only escapes from the end of the tube, but it also falls down to the bottom of the flask like a heavy substance. That's because it is a heavy substance. This is the wax of the candle made into a vaporous fluid, not

15

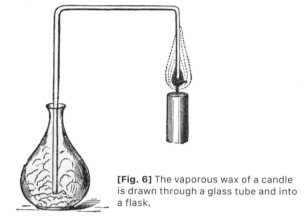

[Fig. 6] The vaporous wax of a candle is drawn through a glass tube and into a flask.

a gas. (You must learn the difference between a gas and a vapor: a gas remains permanent, while a vapor is something that will condense.) If you blow out a candle, you will smell something nasty resulting from the condensation of this vapor. That is different from what you have outside the flame.

In order to make that more clear, I am about to produce and set fire to a larger portion of this vapor. To understand what we observe in a small way in a candle, we must perform experiments in a larger way to examine the different parts so, as scientists, we can understand it thoroughly. Here is some wax in a glass flask. I am going to make it hot, as the inside of a candle flame is hot and the matter around the wick is hot. Now, you see that the wax I put in it has become fluid, and there is a little smoke coming from it. This is exactly the same kind of vapor as we have in the middle of the candle.

Here I arrange another tube carefully in the flame [Fig. 7]. You can see that vapor passes through the tube from one end to the other. When I light it, you can see the flame of the candle at a place distant from it. Is this not a pretty experiment? This shows us that there are clearly two different kinds of action: one is the production of the vapor,

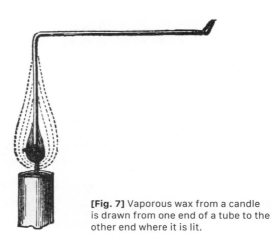

[Fig. 7] Vaporous wax from a candle is drawn from one end of a tube to the other end where it is lit.

and the other is the combustion of it. Both of these take place in particular parts of the candle.

No vapor will come from the part that is already burned. If I raise the tube [fig. 6] to the upper part of the flame where there is no vapor, what comes away will not be combustible because it is already burned. How burned? In the middle of the flame, where the wick is, there is this combustible vapor. On the outside of the flame is the air that is necessary for the burning of the candle. Between the two, intense chemical action takes place, whereby the air and the fuel act upon each other. At the same time that we obtain light, the vapor inside is destroyed.

If you examine where the heat of a candle is, you will find its arrangement curious. Suppose I take this candle and put a piece of paper right across the middle of the flame. Where is the heat of that flame? Do you see that it is not in the inside? Look at the ring-shaped **charring** that appears on one side of the paper. This shows us that the heat is in a ring, exactly in the place where I told you the chemical action was. As long as there is not too much disturbance to the air, there will always be a ring. This is important for you to understand. Air is absolutely necessary for combustion. What's more, you must understand that fresh air is necessary, or else we would have problems with both our reasoning and our experiments.

Here is a jar of air. If I place it over a candle, the candle burns very nicely at first, but there will soon be a change. See how the flame draws upwards, grows weaker, and then, at last, goes out. Why does that happen? It's not because it merely wants air, for the jar is as full now as it was before. Rather, it wants pure, fresh air. The jar is full of air, partly changed, partly not changed, but it does not contain enough fresh air necessary for the combustion of a candle. These are all points that we, as young chemists, have to consider. If we look a little more closely into this kind of action, we shall find certain steps of reasoning extremely interesting. For instance, here I have an oil lamp. I will make it like a candle by only allowing air to reach the outside of the flame, not the center. There is the cotton, which has oil rising up it, and there is the conical flame. Because the air is blocked, it burns poorly. I am unable to allow more air to enter from the outside because the wick is large. But when I open a passage for the air to the middle of the flame, you can see how much more beautifully it burns. If I shut the air out, look how it smokes. Why is this?

We now have some very interesting points to study. We have the case of the combustion of a candle, we have the case of a candle being put out because of a lack of air, and we have the case of **imperfect combustion**. I will now make a great flame because we need the largest possible illustrations to understand this.

Here I am burning **turpentine** on a ball of cotton, which shall be our larger wick. All these things are the same as candles, after all. If we have larger wicks, we must have a larger supply of air, or we shall have less perfect combustion. Now, look at this black substance going up into the atmosphere. There is a regular stream of it. Look at the **soot** that flies off from the flame. You can see what an imperfect combustion it is because it cannot get enough air. What, then, is happening? A few moments ago, you saw the charring of one side of a piece of paper by the ring of flame. If I had shown you the other side of the paper, you would have seen that the burning of a candle produces the same kind of soot: **charcoal** or **carbon**.

Now, when we light a candle, we see that the general result is combustion in the form of a flame. But we must see whether combustion is always like this or whether there are other conditions of the flame. In fact, there are other conditions and they are important to us.

Here is a little **gunpowder**. It contains carbon and other materials, which altogether cause it to burn with a flame. And here are some **iron filings**. We shall burn these two things together. The gunpowder should set fire to the filings, burning them in the air, which will show us the difference between substances burning with flame and without flame. Here is the mixture. When I set fire to it, you will see that it results in two kinds of combustion. Now, what happened? The gunpowder burned with the flame, throwing up the filings. The filings burned separately with a different kind of combustion. This difference is important. When we use oil, gas, or a candle for the purpose of illumination, their suitability all depends upon these different kinds of combustion.

Let us examine another substance to help us distinguish one kind of combustion from another. This is **lycopodium**. It is a powder that is very combustible, and it consists of separate little **particles**. Each of these particles can produce a vapor and its own flame. But when you see it burning, it looks like it's all one flame. Watch as I set fire to it. Did you hear the rushing noise that accompanied the cloud of flame? That is proof that the combustion was not a continuous one or a regular one. This is not an example of combustion like that of the filings I have been speaking of.

Suppose I take a candle and examine the part that appears brightest to our eyes. There I get those black particles, which you have already seen come from the flame many times. I now arrange a glass tube just inside this **luminous** part, higher than it was in our first experiment. You can see the result. In place of having the same white vapor that you had before, you now have a vapor that is black as ink. When we put a light to it, we see that it does not burn. Instead, it puts the light out.

These particles, as I said before, are just the smoke of the candle, and it is the same carbon that exists in the candle. How does it come out? We know it existed in the candle, or else it would not have appeared. And now, I want you to follow my explanation carefully. The soot and other dark matter that fly about London are the very beauty and life of the flame. They are just like the iron filings that we burned a moment ago. Here is a piece of wire gauze, which will not let the flame go through it. You can see that when I bring it low enough to touch the bright part of the flame, the wire gauze puts it out and smoke rises up. Like the iron filings burned in the flame of gunpowder, whenever a substance burns without becoming a vapor (whether it becomes liquid or remains solid), it becomes extremely luminous. This is **applicable** to all substances, whether they burn or whether they do not burn. If they retain their solid state, they become exceedingly bright, so it is the presence of solid particles in the candle flame that gives it its intense brightness.

Here is a platinum wire, a substance that does not change by heat. If I put it in this flame, see how bright it becomes. I will make the flame **dim** so it only gives a little light, but you will see that the heat is still able to bring the platinum wire to a higher state of brightness. This flame has carbon in it, but I will take one that has no carbon in it.

There is a kind of gas in this vessel with no solid particles in it. I use it because it is an example of flame burning without any solid matter. If I now put this solid substance in it, you can see what an intense heat it has and how brightly it causes the solid substance to glow. This is the pipe through which we convey this particular gas, which we call **hydrogen** (we shall discuss this gas the next time we meet). And here is a substance called **oxygen**, which we need to make the hydrogen burn. Although mixing them produces far greater heat than you can obtain from a candle, there is very little light. Here is a piece of **lime**, a solid substance that does not vaporize from heat. If I put the lime into the flame of the hydrogen, we can see an intense light. See how it glows!

Here I have a piece of charcoal, which is a form of carbon that will burn and give us light exactly in the same manner as if it were burned as part of a candle. The heat that is in the flame of a candle breaks down the vapor of the wax, setting free the carbon particles. They rise up heated and glowing, just as this charcoal now glows, and then enter into the air. But when the particles are burned, they never leave the candle in the form of carbon. They go off into the air as a substance we cannot see.

Isn't it beautiful that such a process is going on

and that a thing as dirty as charcoal can become so **incandescent**? This is where our exploration leads. All bright flames contain these solid particles. And all things that burn and produce solid particles, either during the time they are burning, as in the candle, or immediately after being burned, as in the case of the gunpowder and iron filings, give us this glorious and beautiful light.

Here are two substances I have mixed together: **potassium chlorate** and **antimony trisulfide**. I shall touch them with a drop of **sulfuric acid** to give you an illustration of chemical action, and they will instantly burn. You can judge for yourselves whether they produce solid matter. As you must now understand, this bright flame is caused by the solid particles rising up.

When the particles are not separated, you get no brightness. The flame of a candle gets its brightness from the separation of these particles of carbon during combustion. Now, see what happens when I change the conditions. Here is a bright flame of gas. If I add so much air to the flame that it all burns before those particles are set free, I shall not have this brightness. There is plenty of carbon in the gas, but because the atmosphere can get to it and mix with it before it burns, the result is this pale blue flame. And if I blow upon a bright gas flame to make it consume all this carbon before it gets heated to the glowing point, it will also burn blue. The difference is solely due to the solid particles not being separated before the gas is burned.

You have observed today that there are certain products that result from the combustion of a candle, and of these products, one portion may be considered charcoal or soot. Burning that charcoal produces yet another product, and it is important that we see what that other product is. We saw that something was going away, and I want you to understand how much is going up into the air. For that purpose, we will perform combustion on a little larger scale. Here I have a balloon that I will use to try to catch the products of combustion. This plate shall act as the cup of our candle, and this alcohol shall be our fuel. I will place a chimney over it and then light the fuel. I will now hold the balloon over the chimney [Fig. 8]. See how it fills? And when I release the balloon, look how it ascends. Does this help you see how much matter is being produced?

Now, here is another candle, which I will place

under a bell jar. I will put a light behind the jar so that you can see what is going on. Look at how the sides of the jar become cloudy and the light gets weaker. It is the products of the candle that make the light so dim and the sides of the jar **opaque**. If you go home and take a spoon that has been in the cold air and hold it over a candle, you will find that it becomes cloudy, just as that jar is cloudy. And now, just to carry your thoughts forward to the time we shall next meet, let me tell you that it is water that causes the dimness. Next time, I will show you that we can easily make it change into a liquid.

[Fig. 8] A balloon quickly fills with the products of lit alcohol that pass through a chimney.

Lecture III:
The Products of
Combustion

第3講　燃焼による生成物

前回の講義の最後に、ロウソクが燃えたときに出てくる生成物の話をしました。ロウソクがちゃんと燃えているときには得られない物質が一つあって、それは炭や煙でした。そしてもう一つ、炎から上に向かって、煙としてではなく、何か別の形をとって上がっていく物質がありました。

【第3講に出てくる主な用語や表現】

ページ

31	invisible	目に見えない
	condensable	凝縮できる
	incondensable	凝縮できない
	potassium	カリウム
33	gaseous	気体の
34	volume	体積
	convert	転換する
	cast iron	鋳鉄
35	watch glass	時計皿
36	vacuum	真空
	cubic inch[foot]	立法インチ［フィート］
38	furnace	炉
	gun barrel	銃身
39	stopcock	栓
41	elementary substance	単体
42	vial	小瓶
	zinc	亜鉛
	philosopher's candle	賢者のともし火
	soap suds	石けんの泡
44	voltaic pile	ボルタ電池
	composition	組成

We ended our last lecture by talking about the products that come from the candle when it burns. There was one substance that was not obtained when the candle was burning properly, which was charcoal or smoke. And there was another substance that went upward from the flame that did not appear as smoke but took some other form. This **invisible** product joined with the current and ascended from the candle. There were also other products to mention. You remember that in the rising current that came from the candle, we found that one part was **condensable** against a cold spoon, and another part was **incondensable**.

We will first consider the condensable part, which we found was just water. We already performed an experiment that showed us the condensing of water. Next, I will show you a visible action of water. Here is **potassium**, a chemical substance that has a very energetic action upon

water. I shall use this as a test of the presence of
water by taking a little piece of it and throwing it
into that basin. See how it shows the presence of
water by lighting up and floating about, burning
with a violent flame.

I am now going to take away the candle, which
has been burning beneath a vessel containing ice
and salt [Fig. 9]. You can see a drop of water, a
condensed product of the candle, hanging from
under the surface. I will show you that potassium
has the same action upon it as upon the water in

[Fig. 9] A lit candle causes
condensation to appear on the
bottom of a vessel containing
ice and salt.

that basin. See, it takes fire and burns in just the same manner.

Water is one individual thing—it never changes. We can add to it or we can take it apart and get other things from it, but water, as water, always remains the same, either in a solid or liquid state. In this bottle is some water produced by the combustion of an oil lamp. A pint of oil, when burned properly, produces rather more than a pint of water. Here, again, is some water, which was produced by a rather long experiment from a wax candle. And so we can go on with almost all combustible substances and find that if they burn with a flame, as a candle, they produce water.

And now, to go into the history of this wonderful production of water from combustibles, I must first tell you that this water may exist in different conditions. While it can change into different forms, those forms are absolutely the same thing, whether they are produced from a candle, by combustion, or from the rivers or ocean.

The coldest form of water is ice. Now, whether water is in its solid, liquid, or **gaseous** state, we scientists speak of it chemically as water. Water is composed of two substances: we obtained one from the candle and we shall find the other elsewhere. Water may occur as ice, and ice changes back into water when the temperature is raised. Water also changes into steam when it is warmed enough. The water that we have here before us is in its densest state, and although it changes in weight, in condition, in form, and in many other qualities, it still is water. Whether we alter it into ice by cooling or whether we change it into steam by heat, it increases in **volume**, in the first case very strangely and powerfully, and in the second case very largely and wonderfully.

I will now take this tin cylinder and pour a little water into it. I will **convert** the water into steam to show you the different volumes that water occupies in its different states. In the meantime, let us also take the case of water changing into ice. We can achieve that by cooling it in a mixture of salt and pounded ice. I shall do so to show you the expansion of water into a larger volume as it changes. These bottles are made of **cast iron**, and they are very strong and about a third of an inch thick. They are carefully filled with water so as to keep out all air, and then they are tightly closed. We shall see that when we freeze the water in these iron bottles, they will not be able to hold the ice, and the expansion within them will break them to pieces. The water in the bottles and the ice outside shall never meet, but the heat shall transfer from one to the other. I will put them here into the mixture of ice and salt.

Now, look at the change that has taken place in the water to which we have applied heat. It is losing its fluid state. You can observe this in several ways. I have covered the mouth of the cylinder with a **watch glass**. You can see it rattling because the steam rising from the boiling water is forcing itself out. You can also see that the volume of water has not significantly decreased, which shows you that the change in volume is very great when it becomes steam. Now, see what a stream of vapor is coming out of the bottle! We must have made it quite full of steam to have it sent out in that great quantity. And now, as we can convert the water into steam by heat, we convert it back into liquid water by the application of cold. And if we take a glass, or any other cold thing, and hold it over this steam, see how soon it gets damp with water. It will condense it until the glass is warm—it condenses the water that is now running down the sides of it.

Here I have another experiment to show the condensation of water from a vaporous state back into a liquid state, just as the vapor from the candle was condensed against the bottom of the dish. I will take this tin flask, which is now full of steam, and close the top. We shall see what takes place when we cause this water or steam to return to the fluid state by pouring some cold water on the outside [Fig. 10]. You see what has happened. If I had closed the stopper and still kept the heat applied to it, it would have burst the flask. But when the steam returns to the state of water, the flask collapses because of the **vacuum** produced inside the flask by the condensation of the steam. I show you these experiments to point out that in all these occurrences, there is nothing that changes the water into any other thing—it still remains water.

And what do you think the volume of that water is when it assumes the vaporous condition? A **cubic inch** of water is sufficient to expand into a **cubic foot** of steam [Fig. 11]. And the application of cold will contract a large quantity of steam into a small quantity of water.

Ah! One of our bottles just burst. You can see

[Fig. 10] A flask full of steam collapses as cold water poured on the outside of the flask produces a vacuum on the inside as the steam changes to water.

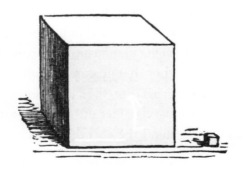

[Fig. 11] A cubic inch of water can expand to a cubic foot of steam.

a crack down one side an eighth of an inch in width. And there goes the other bottle. Although the iron was nearly half an inch thick, the ice has made it burst. These changes frequently take place naturally in water in colder climates. Now, you know very well that ice floats on water. Why does the ice float? Because the ice is larger than the quantity of water that can produce it, and therefore the ice is lighter and the water is heavier.

Now then, we will no longer be deceived by any changes that are produced in water. Water is the same everywhere, whether it's produced from the ocean or from the flame of the candle. Where, then, is this water that we get from a candle? Part of it evidently comes from the candle, but is it within the candle beforehand? No. It is not in the candle, and it is not in the air around the candle that is necessary for its combustion. It is neither in one nor the other, but it comes from their combined action: a part from the candle and a part from the air. We must consider this so that we may thoroughly understand the chemical history of a candle.

Here I have a **furnace** with a pipe going through it like an iron **gun barrel**, and I have stuffed it full of iron that will turn red hot from the fire. We can either send air through the barrel to come in contact with the iron, or we can send steam from this little boiler at the end of the barrel [Fig. 12]. Here is a **stopcock**, which shuts off the steam from the barrel until we wish to let it in. There is some water in these glass cylinders, which I have colored blue, so that you may see what happens. Now, if I sent steam through the barrel and it also went through the water, it would be condensed. You know this because you have seen that steam cannot retain its gaseous form when it is cooled down.

[Fig. 12] Passing steam through a furnace and then water results in the production of a certain type of gas.

I am going to send the steam through the barrel in small quantities, and you shall judge for yourselves whether it still remains steam when you see it come out of the other end. Steam is condensable into water, and when you lower the temperature of steam, you convert it back into fluid water. But I have lowered the temperature of the gas that I have collected in this jar by passing it through water after it went through the iron barrel, and still it does not change back into water.

If I now bring a taper to the mouth of the jar, it ignites with a slight noise. That tells you that it is not steam. Steam puts out a fire—it does not burn. But the substance in the jar burned. We may obtain this substance equally from water produced from the candle flame as from any other source. As we have another jar full of the same gas, I will show you something interesting. It is a combustible gas, but it is also a very light substance. Steam will condense, but this substance will rise in the air without condensing.

Suppose I take another glass jar that is only filled with air. If I examine it with this flame, we can see that it contains nothing but air. I will now take this jar full of the gas that I am speaking of and deal with it as though it were a light substance. I will hold both upside down and turn one up under the other [Fig. 13]. Consider the jar that contained the gas we obtained from the steam. What does it contain now? You will find it now only contains air. But look! Here in the other jar is the combustible substance that I have poured out of one jar into the other. It still preserves its quality, condition, and independence.

Let us now carefully consider the relationship between these two points. This is hydrogen, which chemistry describes as an element because we can get nothing else out of it. A candle is not an **elementary substance** because we can get carbon

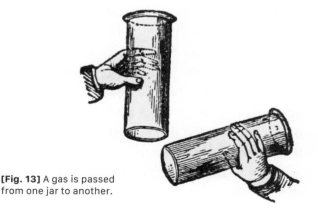

[Fig. 13] A gas is passed from one jar to another.

out of it. We can also get this hydrogen out of it, or at least out of the water that it supplies. And this gas is called hydrogen because it is the element that generates water when combined with another element.

This hydrogen is a very beautiful substance. It is so light that it carries things up. It is far lighter than the atmosphere, which I will show you in this experiment. For our purposes, we will use this curious instrument. You see that there is a **vial** with a cork and a tube passing through it. Inside the vial are some bits of **zinc** in sulfuric acid, which is producing hydrogen for us. If I were to light the end, we would observe hydrogen burning. This is what's known as a "**philosopher's candle**" [Fig. 14].

Now, here are some **soap suds**. I have a rubber tube connected to the hydrogen generator, and at the end of the tube is a tobacco pipe. I can put a pipe into the suds and blow bubbles by means of the hydrogen. Observe how the bubbles fall downwards when I blow them with my warm breath, but notice the difference when I blow them with hydrogen. It shows you how light this gas must be in order to carry with it not only the ordinary soap bubble but also the larger portion of a drop of water hanging to the bottom of it.

Hydrogen gives rise to no substance that can become solid, either during combustion or afterward as a product of its combustion. But when it burns, it produces water only, and if we take a cold glass and put it over the flame, it becomes damp with water. Nothing produced by its combustion but the same water that you have seen the flame of the candle produce. It is important to remember that this hydrogen is the only thing in nature that furnishes water as the sole product of combustion.

[Fig. 14] A philosopher's candle is made by lighting the end of a vial containing zinc in sulfuric acid to produce hydrogen.

Now, we have previously seen the power of combustion of potassium, zinc, and iron filings, but I will show you something with much more power. I have behind me a **voltaic pile**, which is a sort of battery. Here are the ends of two wires that will transport the power from the battery, and its power is great—as great as several thunderstorms. In our next lecture, I shall apply it to water so that we may learn more about its character and **composition**.

Lecture IV:
Hydrogen and Oxygen

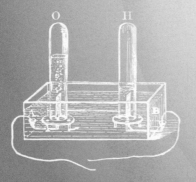

第4講　水素と酸素

　前回の講義では、ロウソクが燃えると、水が作られること
を学びました。さらに調べると、水の中には水素という軽い
元素が含まれていること、また水素が燃えて水だけを発生
させることもわかりました。では、水の中に存在するもう一
つの物質が何であるかを見てみましょう。

【第4講に出てくる主な用語や表現】

ページ

47	pole	電極
	apparatus	装置, 器具
48	pile	電池
49	inverted	（上下が）逆さまの
	splinter	細片
	electrolysis	電気分解
	diagram	図表
50	manganese oxide	酸化マンガン
	oxide	酸化物
	mineral	鉱物
	potassium chlorate	塩素酸カリウム
	bleaching	漂白
	pyrotechnic	花火
51	diluted	薄められた
	property	性質
	transparent	透明な
	undissolved	溶解されていない
52	phenomena	《複》現象
53	decompose	分解する
54	confined	限られた

Now, we shall see what the other substance present in water is. Suppose I take the **poles** of this battery, which are the metallic ends, and see what will happen with the water in this **apparatus** [Fig. 15], where we have separated the two ends far apart. I

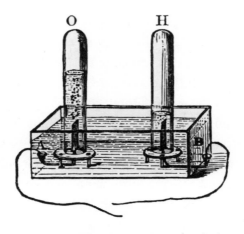

[Fig. 15] A battery causes water to separate into hydrogen and oxygen gases.

47

place one here (at A) and the other there (at B), and I have little stands with holes that I can put upon each pole. Whatever escapes from the two ends of the battery will appear here as separate gases.

The wires are now connected, and you can see the bubbles rising. Let us collect these bubbles and see what they are. Here is a glass cylinder (O). I fill it with water and put it over one end (A) of the **pile**. I will take another (H) and put it over the other end (B) of the pile. And so now we have a double apparatus, with both places delivering gas. Both these cylinders will fill with gas. You can see the one on the right (H) filling very rapidly and the one to the left (O) filling not so rapidly. Observe that there is twice as much in this (H) as I have in that (O). Both these gases are colorless, and they stand over the water without condensing. They are alike in all things—I mean in all apparent things—and we have here an opportunity to examine these substances to find out what they are. Their volume is large, and we can easily apply experiments to them. I will take this cylinder (H) first, which you shall soon recognize as hydrogen.

If this is indeed hydrogen, it will remain here

while I hold the cylinder **inverted**. And if I put flame to it, see how it lights. Now, what is in the other cylinder? We know that the water we put into the vessel consisted of the two substances together. I am about to put this lighted **splinter** of wood into the gas. The gas itself will not burn, but it will make the splinter of wood burn.

See how it gives strength to the combustion of the wood. It makes it burn far better than the air would make it burn. Now, you see that the other substance that is contained in the water must be taken from the atmosphere when the candle burns. This, then, is the oxygen.

We shall now begin to understand our experiments and research more clearly because we will see why a candle burns in the air. When we have analyzed the water like this using **electrolysis** to separate it, we get two volumes of hydrogen and one volume of the substance that burns it. And these two are represented to us in the following **diagram**, with their weights also stated. We shall find that oxygen is a very heavy substance compared to hydrogen.

I had better, perhaps, tell you now how we get this oxygen abundantly, as I have already shown you how we can separate it from the water. Oxygen, as you will immediately imagine, exists in the atmosphere, for how could the candle burn to produce water without it?

1 Hydrogen	8 Oxygen / 9

Oxygen.........................88.9
Hydrogen....................11.1
_____
Water..........................100.0

Such a thing would be chemically impossible without oxygen.

Can we get oxygen from the air? Well, there are some very complicated and difficult processes by which we can, but we have a better way. There is a substance called **manganese oxide**. It is a very black-looking **mineral**, and when made red hot, it gives out oxygen. Here is an iron bottle that has some of this substance in it, and there is a tube fixed to it [Fig. 16]. I shall put the bottle into this fire, for it is made of iron so it can stand the heat. Here is a salt called **potassium chlorate**, which is now made in large quantities for **bleaching**, and chemical and medical uses, and for **pyrotechnic** and other purposes. I will take some and mix it

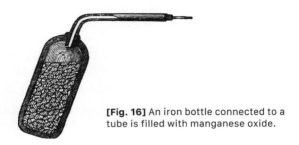

[Fig. 16] An iron bottle connected to a tube is filled with manganese oxide.

with some of the manganese oxide. If I put these together in a bottle, far less than a red heat is enough to produce oxygen from the mixture. But, as you will see immediately, if I use too small an amount, the first portion of the gas will be mixed with the air already in the bottle, and I would have to throw away the first portion of the gas because it would be so **diluted** with air. In this case, you will find that a common alcohol burner is quite sufficient for me to get the oxygen, and so we shall have two processes going on for its preparation.

See how freely the gas is coming over from that small portion of the mixture. We will examine it and see what its **properties** are. Now, in this way, we are producing a gas just like the one we had in the experiment with the battery, **transparent**, **undissolved** by water, and exhibiting the ordinary visible properties of the atmosphere. And we should expect it to exhibit the same power of making things burn. We will try it. As I lower this taper [Fig. 17] into the jar, see how brightly and how beautifully it burns! You can also see that it is a heavy gas. If it were hydrogen, it would go up like a balloon.

You may easily see that although we obtained from water twice as much in volume of the hydrogen as of the oxygen, it does not follow that we have twice as much in weight. After all, one is heavy, and the other a very light gas.

Now, we shall compare the property of oxygen supporting combustion to that of air. Here is a candle burning in air. And here I have a jar of oxygen that I will now put over the candle for you to compare. Why, look at how bright it is! And yet, during all that action, we have the same production of water and exactly the same **phenomena** as when we use air. It is wonderful how great the supporting powers

[Fig. 17] A lighted taper is prepared to be lowered into a gas.

of this substance are as regards combustion.

I am now going to set fire to oxygen and hydrogen, mixed in the proportion in which they occur in water. Here is a vessel containing one volume of oxygen and two volumes of hydrogen. I will blow soap bubbles with it and burn those bubbles so we may see how the oxygen supports the combustion of the hydrogen. Now, here is a bubble, and I shall let it land on my hand. You might think I am acting strange in this experiment. The truth is I am afraid to fire a bubble at the end of the pipe because the explosion would pass up into the jar and blow it to pieces.

Now, I have exploded a bubble in the palm of my hand. This oxygen then will unite with the hydrogen, as you see by the phenomena and hear by the sound. So now, I think you understand the whole history of water with reference to oxygen and the air.

Why does a piece of potassium **decompose** water? Because it finds oxygen in the water. What is set free when I put it in the water, as I am about to do again? It sets free hydrogen, and the hydrogen burns, but the potassium itself combines with oxygen. This piece of potassium, in taking the water apart, takes away the oxygen that the candle took from the air, setting the hydrogen free. Even if I take a piece of ice and put some potassium upon it, the ice will absolutely set fire to the potassium. Here is the potassium on the ice, producing a sort of volcanic action.

The next time we meet, I must show you that we see none of these strange and dangerous actions take place when we are burning not merely a candle but also gas in our streets or fuel in our fireplaces. These actions are **confined** by the laws governed by nature.

Lecture V:
The Nature of
the Atmosphere

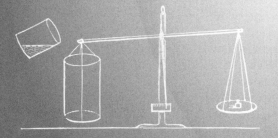

第5講 大気の正体

　ここまでで、ロウソクから得られる水から、水素と酸素を生成できることがわかりました。水素はロウソクから、酸素は空気から発生します、それならどうして空気と酸素の中では、ロウソクの燃え方が違うのでしょうか。その答えは、大気の性質に関係しているのです。

【第5講に出てくる主な用語や表現】

ページ

58	creep	ゆっくり動く
	our test gas	一酸化二窒素のこと
59	nitrogen	窒素
60	dissolve	溶ける
	alkali	アルカリ
	indifferent	（反応に対して）中性の
	grate	炉の火格子
61	mass	質量
62	balance	てんびん
63	air inlet	吸気口
64	bladder	ぼうこう
	hemisphere	半球（体）
65	suction cup	吸着カップ
66	resistance	抵抗
68	elasticity	弾性
	compressibility	圧縮性
	expansibility	膨張性
70	chalk	チョーク
	limestone	石灰岩［石］
71	carbon dioxide	二酸化炭素
	muriatic acid	塩酸
72	carbonate	炭酸塩

We have now seen that we can produce hydrogen and oxygen from the water that we obtained from the candle. Hydrogen, you know, comes from the candle, and oxygen, you believe, comes from the air. But then you have a right to ask me, "How is it that the air and the oxygen do not burn the candle equally well?" If you remember what happened when I put a jar of oxygen over a piece of candle, there was a very different kind of combustion from the combustion that took place in the air. Why is this? The answer relates to the nature of the atmosphere.

We have several tests for oxygen besides just burning different materials. You have seen a candle burned in oxygen and in the air, and you have seen iron filings burned in oxygen. I am about to perform some more tests to broaden your understanding. Here are two jars that are full of gas with a plate between them to prevent their mixing. I take the plate away, and the gases **creep** one into the other. What's happening? They do not combust, but what a beautifully red-colored gas I have obtained! This shows us the presence of oxygen.

In the same way, we can try this experiment by mixing ordinary air with this test gas. Here is a jar containing air, such air as the candle would burn in, and here is a jar containing the test gas. I let them come together over water and you see the result: the contents of the test bottle are flowing into the jar of air, and you see I obtain exactly the same kind of action as before. That shows me that there is oxygen in the air, the very same substance that we have already obtained from the water produced by the candle. But how is it that the candle does not burn in air as well as in oxygen? We will come to that point at once.

Here are two jars filled to the same height with gas. They look exactly alike, and I do not know which of the jars contains oxygen and which of the jars contains air. But here is **our test gas**, which we will use to examine whether there is any difference in how red the gases become. I am now going to release this test gas into one of the jars. There is reddening, you see, so there is oxygen present. We will now test the other jar, but you see that it is not as red as the first, and further, a curious thing happens. If I take these two gases and shake them well together with water, we shall absorb the red gas. And then, if I put in more of this test gas and shake again, we shall absorb more. And I can go on as long as there is any oxygen present to produce that effect. If I let in air, it will not matter, but the moment I introduce water, the red gas disappears. I can continue like this, putting in more and more of the test gas, until I'm left with something that will not redden any longer. Why is that? It is because there is, besides oxygen, something else present that is left behind. This something is not oxygen, and yet it is part of the atmosphere.

So that is one way of separating air into the two things of which it is composed: oxygen, which burns our candles or anything else, and this other substance, **nitrogen**, which will not burn them. This other part of the air is by far the larger proportion, and it is very curious, although you might think that it is very uninteresting. Indeed, it is uninteresting in some respects because it does not combust. If I test it with a taper as I do oxygen and hydrogen, it does not burn like hydrogen, nor does it make the taper burn like oxygen. Rather, it puts out the combustion of everything. There is nothing that will burn in it in common circumstances. It has no smell, it has no taste, it does not **dissolve** in water, it is neither an acid nor an **alkali**, and it is as **indifferent** to all our organs as possible.

And you might say, "It is nothing. It is not worth chemical attention. What does it do in the air?" Ah! Let us consider what science has to say. Suppose, in place of having nitrogen, or nitrogen and oxygen, we had pure oxygen as our atmosphere. What would happen to us? You know very well that a piece of iron lit in a jar of oxygen goes on burning to the end. When you see a fire in an iron **grate**, imagine what would happen if the whole atmosphere were oxygen. The grate would burn up more powerfully than the coals, for the iron of the grate itself is even more combustible than the coals that we burn in it. A fire put into the middle of a locomotive would go out of control if the atmosphere were oxygen. The nitrogen lowers it down and makes it moderate and useful for us, and then it carries away the fumes that you have seen produced from the candle into the atmosphere.

This nitrogen, in its ordinary state, is an inactive element. No action short of the most intense and focused electric force can cause nitrogen to combine directly with other elements in the atmosphere or with other things around it. It is a perfectly indifferent and, therefore, safe substance.

But before we consider that, I must tell you about the atmosphere itself. I have written here the composition of one hundred parts of atmospheric air:

	Volume	Mass
Oxygen	20	22.3
Nitrogen	80	77.7
	100	100

By our analysis, we find that 5 parts of the atmosphere contain only 1 part of oxygen and 4 parts of nitrogen by volume. It requires all that quantity of nitrogen to reduce the oxygen enough to supply the candle properly with fuel and supply us with an atmosphere that our lungs can healthily and safely breathe.

But now for this atmosphere. First of all, let me tell you the weight of these gases. Two liters of nitrogen gas weigh roughly 2.29 grams. The oxygen is heavier. Two liters of oxygen gas weigh around 2.62 grams. Two liters of air weigh about 2.37 grams.[1]

But how do you weigh gases? Here is a **balance**, and here is a perfectly air-tight copper bottle with a stopcock, which we can open and shut. Here is a nicely-adjusted balance, with the bottle balanced by the weight on the other side. And here is a pump we can use to force the air into the bottle [Fig. 18]. I will pump it twenty times, shut it, and place it on the balance. See how it sinks. It is much heavier than it was because of the air that we have forced into it with the pump. There is not a greater volume of air, but there is the same volume

[Fig. 18] A pump is used to force air into a vessel.

---

[1] Hammack, W.S., & DeCoste, D.J. (2016). Michael Faraday's The Chemical History of a Candle. Urbana, Illinois: Articulate Noise Books.

of heavier air because we have forced air into it. It is wonderful how it accumulates when you come to larger volumes. I have calculated the weight of the air in this room. You might not believe it, but it is more than a ton.

Now that we've gained an understanding of the weight of the air, let me show you its significance. Suppose I take a pump somewhat similar to the one I used to force air into the bottle. What happens when I pump out the air and put my hand against the **air inlet**? Why is my hand fastened to this place, and why am I able to pull this pump about? It is because of the weight of the air outside the pump [Fig. 19].

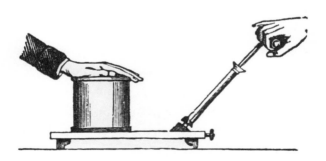

[Fig. 19] A pump draws air through an air inlet, causing the inlet to fasten to a hand.

I have another experiment here that will help you understand. When the air is pumped from underneath the **bladder** that is stretched over this glass, you will see the same effect in another way. The top is now quite flat, but I force air out of the glass with the pump, and now look at it. See how the bladder has gone down. See how it is bent into the glass. You will see the bladder go in more and more until, at last, I expect it will be driven in and broken by the force of the atmosphere pressing upon it. There it goes. That was done entirely by the weight of the air pressing on it, and you can easily understand how that is. The particles that are piled up in the atmosphere stand upon each other, as these five blocks here do [Fig. 20]. You can easily see that four of these five blocks are resting upon the bottom one, and if I take that away, the others will all sink down. So it is with the atmosphere. The air that is above is sustained by the air that is beneath, and when the air is pumped away from beneath them, the change occurs that you saw when I placed my hand on the air pump and when the bladder went down into the glass.

Now, here is a little apparatus of two hollow brass **hemispheres**, closely fitted together. They are

[Fig. 20] Like blocks, particles in the atmosphere stand upon each other.

connected to a pipe and a stopcock through which we can exhaust the air from the inside. Although the two halves are easily taken apart while there is air inside, you will see that when the air is taken out, none of you will be able to pull them apart. The pressure on every square inch of the vessel is about fifteen pounds when the air is taken out.

Here is another pretty thing: a **suction cup** made of rubber. If I clap it upon the table, you see it holds at once. Why does it hold? I can slide it around from place to place, and yet if I try to pull it up, it seems as if it would pull the table with it. Only when I bring it to the edge of the table can I get it off. It is only kept down by the pressure of the atmosphere above. We have a couple of them, and if you take these two and press them together, you will see how firmly they stick. And, indeed, we may use them as they are proposed to be used, to stick against windows or against walls, where they will adhere for an evening and serve to hang anything that you want.

I will show you another experiment concerning the pressure of the atmosphere. Here is a glass of water. Suppose I were to ask you to turn that glass upside down without letting the water out using the pressure of the atmosphere rather than your hand. Could you do that? Put a flat card on the top, turn it upside down, and then see what becomes of the card and of the water. The air cannot get in because the water, by its capillary action around the edge, keeps it out.

I will conduct another experiment to convince you of the positive **resistance** of air. There is a beautiful experiment of a popgun, made so well and so easily out of a tube. We can take a piece of this potato, as I have done, and push it to one end of the tube. I have made the end tight. And now, I take another piece and put it in. It will confine the air that is within the tube perfectly and completely for our purpose. And I shall now find it absolutely impossible by any force of mine to drive that little piece close up to the other. It cannot be done. I may press the air to a certain extent, but if I go on pressing, the confined air will drive the front one out with a force something like that of gunpowder long before one piece comes to the other. Gunpowder, you see, is in part dependent upon the same action that you see here.

The other day, I saw this next experiment, which I thought would serve our purpose here. By the proper application of air, I expect to be able to drive this egg out of one cup and into the other by the force of my breath. If I fail, it is because I have been talking more than I ought to do to make the experiment succeed. There it goes. You see that the air that I blow goes downward between the egg and the cup, and it makes a blast under the egg. Thus, it is able to lift a heavy thing, for a full egg is a very heavy thing for air to lift. If you want to do the experiment yourself, you had better boil the egg quite hard first, and then you may very safely try to blow it from one cup to the other.

We have now discussed the property of the

weight of the air at length, but there is another thing I would like to mention. In this popgun, you saw the way in which I was able to drive the second piece of potato half or two-thirds of an inch before the first piece started, by virtue of the **elasticity** of the air. Similarly, I pressed into the copper bottle the particles of air by means of the pump. Now, this depends upon a wonderful property in the air—namely, its elasticity—and I would like to give you a good illustration of this. I can take something that confines the air, like this bladder, which also is able to contract and expand like a balloon so as to give us a measure of the elasticity of the air. Here I have a bell jar into which I shall place the closed bladder. If I use a pump to take the atmosphere out of the jar, you will see how the bladder will then go on expanding and expanding, larger and larger, until it will fill the bell jar. Now, you can see well the **compressibility** and **expansibility** of the air. Its elasticity is indeed essential for many of the basic functions of life itself.

We will now turn to another very important part of our subject, remembering that we have examined the candle in its burning and have found that it gives rise to various products. We have the products, you know, of soot, of water, and of something else which you have not yet examined. We have collected the water but have allowed the other things to go into the air. Let us now examine some of these other products.

Here is an experiment that I think will help you. We will put our candle there and place a chimney over it like this. I think my candle will go on burning because the air passage is open at the bottom and the top. You can already see moisture appearing—you already know that water is produced from the action of the air upon the candle's hydrogen. But, besides that, something is going out through the top. It is not moisture, it is not water, and it is not condensable. But it has unique properties. You will find that the air coming out of the top of our chimney is nearly sufficient to blow out the flame I am holding near it. And if I put the flame directly into the current, it will blow it right out [Fig. 21]. You may say that is as it should be because the nitrogen does not support combustion and ought to put the candle out since the candle will not burn in nitrogen.

But is there nothing else there besides nitrogen? I will show you how we can determine such a

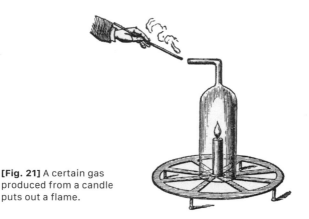

[Fig. 21] A certain gas produced from a candle puts out a flame.

thing. First, I will take this empty jar and hold it over the chimney, thus sending the results of the combustion of the candle below into the bottle above. Then, I will pour some lime water into the jar, and there, do you see that the water has become quite milky? We have made **chalk**, which consists of the lime that is used to make lime water and something that came from the candle. This will not happen with just air. Here is a bottle filled with air, and if I put a little lime water into it, neither the oxygen nor the nitrogen nor anything else that is in that air will make any change in the lime water.

All **limestones** contain a great deal of this gas that issues from the candle and which we call

carbon dioxide. All chalks, all shells, and all corals contain a great quantity of this curious substance. We can easily get this gas from marble. Here is a jar containing a little **muriatic acid**, and here is a taper that will show only the presence of ordinary air if I put it into that jar. There is, you see, pure air down to the bottom—the jar is full of it. Here are some pieces of marble, and if I put them into the jar, a great boiling apparently goes on. That, however, is not steam; it is a gas that is rising up. And if I now place a candle into the jar, you will see exactly the same effect we produced with the bell jar. It is exactly the same action, and it is caused by the very same substance that came from the candle. In this way, we can get carbon dioxide in great abundance.

We also find that this gas is not merely contained in marble. Here is a large jar in which I have put some ordinary chalk, and here I have some strong sulfuric acid. Here you will have just the same kind of action. In this large jar, I am producing carbon dioxide, exactly the same in its nature and properties as the gas that we obtained from the combustion of the candle in the atmosphere. And no matter how different the two methods are that we use to prepare this carbon dioxide, you will see that the result is exactly the same.

We will now proceed to the next experiment with regard to this gas. What is its nature? This vessel is full of the gas, and we will test whether it is combustible. You see, it is not, nor does it support combustion. Neither, as we know, does it dissolve much in water because we collect it over water very easily. Then, you know that it has an effect and becomes white in contact with lime water; and when it does become white in that way, it becomes one of the parts to make **carbonate** of lime or limestone.

The next thing I must show you is that it really does dissolve a little in water, and, therefore, that it is unlike oxygen and hydrogen in that respect. I have here an apparatus by which we can produce this solution. In the lower part of this apparatus is marble and acid, and in the upper part is cold water. The valves are arranged so that the gas can get from one to the other. I will set it in action now, and you can see the gas bubbling up through the water. If I take a glass and draw off some of the water, I find that it has an acidic taste because it is full of carbon dioxide. And if I now apply a little lime water to it, that will give us a test of its presence. This water will make the lime water cloudy and white, which is proof of the presence of carbon dioxide.

Carbon dioxide is a heavy gas, and it is heavier than the atmosphere. In this table, I have put the weights of all the gases we have been examining.

Mass in grams of two liters of various gases[2]

hydrogen	0.16 g
nitrogen	2.29 g
air	2.37 g
oxygen	2.62 g
carbon dioxide	3.60 g

Two liters of this weigh about 3.6 grams. You can see from many experiments that this is a heavy gas. Suppose I take a glass containing nothing else but air, and I attempt to pour a little of this gas from the vessel containing the carbon dioxide into that glass. I wonder whether any has gone in or not. I cannot tell by the appearance, but I can by introducing the taper [Fig. 22]. Yes, there it is—the

---

[2] Hammack, W.S., & DeCoste, D.J. (2016). Michael Faraday's The Chemical History of a Candle. Urbana, Illinois: Articulate Noise Books.

flame has gone out. If I were to examine it using lime water, I would find it by that test also.

There is another experiment that will allow me to show you its weight. Here I have a jar containing just air suspended on one end of a balance. But

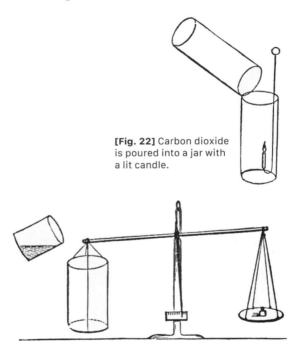

[Fig. 22] Carbon dioxide is poured into a jar with a lit candle.

[Fig. 23] Carbon dioxide poured into a jar on one side of a balance causes that side to sink.

when I pour this carbon dioxide into the jar, you will see it sink down immediately [Fig. 23]. And now, if I examine this jar with the lighted taper, I shall find that the carbon dioxide has fallen into it, and it no longer has the power to support combustion. If I blow a soap bubble, which, of course, will be filled with air, and let it fall into this jar of carbon dioxide, it will float.

I shall now take one of these little balloons filled with air. There, you see, we have this balloon floating on the carbon dioxide. And if I produce some more of the carbon dioxide, the balloon will be lifted up higher. There it goes—the jar is nearly full. I will see whether I can blow a soap bubble on that and float it in the same way. Yes, it is floating, as the balloon floated, by virtue of the greater weight of the carbon dioxide than of the air. And now that you have an understanding of the history of carbon dioxide, when we next meet, I shall show you what it is composed of and where it gets its elements from.

Lecture VI:
Respiration and
its Analogy to the Burning
of a Candle

第6講　呼吸とロウソクの燃焼との関係

　前回は二酸化炭素のことを話しました。ロウソクの上からの蒸気をびんに受けて、石灰水の溶液で検査すると、乳白色になることがわかりました。今度は、ロウソクの働きによって作られた二酸化炭素の元素がどこからくるのかについて見ていきましょう。

【第6講に出てくる主な用語や表現】

ページ

77	respiration	呼吸
	analogy	類似（点）
79	calcareous	石灰質の
81	interfere	じゃまをする
	subsequent	次の
	phosphorus	リン
83	calcium carbonate	炭酸カルシウム
84	carbonaceous	炭素（質）の
	carbonaceous series	炭素質系の物質
	groove	溝
86	external air	外気
87	expired air	呼気
89	sustenance	（生命の）維持
90	oxidize	酸化させる
	oxidizer	酸化剤
91	respire	呼吸する
	kingdom	〜界
92	lead	鉛
	chemical affinity	化学親和力
93	Herculaneum	ヘルクラネウム《古代都市名》
	alteration	変更
	guncotton	綿火薬

When we last met, I told you a good deal about carbon dioxide. We found that when the vapor from the top of the candle was received into bottles and tested by this solution of lime water, it turned milky white. That was a **calcareous** matter, like shells and corals, and many of the rocks and minerals in the earth. But I have not yet told you fully and clearly the chemical history of this substance—carbon dioxide—as we have it from the candle, so I must now resume that subject. We have seen the products and the nature of them as they issue from the candle. We have traced the water to its elements, and now we have to see where the elements of the carbon dioxide supplied by the candle are.

You remember that when a candle burns badly, it produces smoke, but if it is burning well, there is no smoke. And you know that the brightness of the candle is due to this smoke, which becomes ignited. Here is an experiment to prove this. As long as the smoke remains in the flame of the candle and becomes ignited, it gives a beautiful light and never appears to us in the form of black particles. I will light some fuel, which will burn with a strong flame. We will use a little turpentine on a sponge. You see the smoke rising from it and floating into the air in large quantities. Remember now, the carbon dioxide that we produce from the candle is from the same kind of smoke.

To make that clear to you, I will put this turpentine burning on the sponge into a flask where I have plenty of oxygen. You now see that the smoke is all consumed. The carbon that you saw flying off from the turpentine flame in the air is now entirely burned in this oxygen. This gives us exactly the same conclusion and result as we had from the combustion of the candle. All the carbon that is burned in oxygen or air comes out as carbon dioxide, while those particles that are not so burned show you carbon, the second substance in the carbon dioxide. It is this substance that made the flame so bright while there was plenty of air but which was thrown off in excess when there was not enough oxygen to burn it.

There is another experiment that we must perform to increase our understanding of the general nature of carbon dioxide. Because it is a compound substance, consisting of carbon and oxygen, we should be able to separate the two parts. The simplest and quickest way is to use a substance that can attract the oxygen from it and leave the carbon behind. You recall that I took potassium and put it on water and ice, and you saw that it could take the oxygen from the hydrogen. Now, suppose we do something of the same kind here with this carbon dioxide. You know carbon dioxide is a heavy gas. I will not test it with lime water, as that will **interfere** with our **subsequent** experiments, but I think the heaviness of the gas and the power of extinguishing flame will be sufficient for our purpose. I introduce a flame into the gas, and you will see whether it will be put out. You see the light is extinguished. Indeed, the gas may, perhaps, put out **phosphorus**, which has a pretty strong combustion. Here is a piece of phosphorus heated to a high degree. I introduce it into gas, and you observe the light is put out, but it will light up again in the air because there it re-enters into combustion.

Now, here is a piece of potassium. If we warm it up to the burning point in air, as we have done with phosphorus, you will see that it can burn in carbon dioxide. And if it burns, it will burn by taking oxygen, so you will see what is left behind. I am going to burn this potassium in the carbon dioxide as proof of the existence of oxygen in the carbon dioxide. Now that it is heated, I introduce it into the jar, and you see that it burns in the carbon dioxide—not as well as in the air because the carbon dioxide contains the oxygen combined, but it does burn and take away the oxygen. If I now put this potassium into water, I find that there is a quantity of carbon produced. Here, then, is the carbon obtained from the carbon dioxide, as a common black substance, so that you have the entire proof of the nature of carbon dioxide as consisting of carbon and oxygen.

And now, I may tell you that whenever carbon burns under common circumstances, it produces carbon dioxide. Suppose I take this piece of wood and put it into a bottle with lime water and air. No matter how much I shake it up, it will still remain clear. But suppose I burn the piece of wood in the air of that bottle. Of course, you know that I get water. But do I get carbon dioxide? There it is, you see—this is **calcium carbonate**, which results from carbon dioxide, and that carbon dioxide must be formed from carbon, which comes from the wood. Indeed, you have all frequently performed a very pretty experiment that shows the carbon in wood. If you take a piece of wood, partly burn it, and then blow it out, you have carbon left.

There are things that do not show carbon in this way. A candle does not show it, but it contains carbon. I will light this candle, and as long as there is any gas in this cylinder, it will go on burning. You see no carbon, but you see a flame, and because that is bright, it will lead you to guess that there is carbon in the flame. I hope that through these experiments, you will learn to see when carbon is present and understand what the products of combustion are when gas or other substances are thoroughly burned in the air.

Before we leave the subject of carbon, let us perform a few experiments and make some remarks on its wonderful condition in comparison to ordinary combustion. I have shown you that carbon burns only as a solid substance, and yet you know that after it is burned, it is no longer a solid. There are very few fuels that act like this. It is, as far as I know, the only great source of fuel— the **carbonaceous series**, which includes coals, charcoals, and woods—that can burn with these conditions.

And if carbon did not burn in such a way, what would happen to us? Suppose all fuel were like iron, which, when it burns, burns into a solid substance. Then we could not have the combustion you see in a fireplace. If, when the carbon burned, the product went off as a solid substance, it would make the inside of a room opaque. But when carbon burns, everything goes up into the atmosphere. It is in a fixed, almost unchangeable condition before the combustion, but afterward, it is in the form of gas.

Now, let us consider the relationship between the combustion of a candle and the living kind of combustion that goes on within us. Here is a board and a **groove** cut in it, and I can close the groove at the top part with a little cover. I can then continue the groove as a channel by a glass tube at each end, making a free passage from one end to the other [Fig. 24]. Suppose I take a candle and place it in one of the tubes. As you see, it will go on burning very well. You observe that the air that feeds the flame

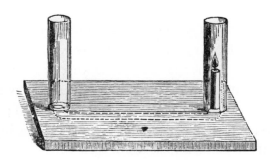

[Fig. 24] Two tubes, one of which contains a lit candle, are connected by a channel.

passes down the tube at one end, then goes along the channel and ascends through the tube at the other end in which the candle is placed.

If I cover the opening through which the air enters, I stop combustion, and, as you see, the candle goes out. But if you recall, in a former experiment [Lecture V, Fig. 21] I showed you the air going from a burning candle to a taper. If I took the air proceeding from another candle and sent it down into this tube, I would put this burning candle out.

Now, what will you say when I tell you that my breath will put out that candle? I do not mean by blowing it out, but simply that the nature of my breath is such that a candle cannot burn in it. I will now hold my mouth over the opening, and without blowing the flame in any way, I will let no air enter the tube except for what comes from my mouth. You see the result. I did not blow the candle out. I merely let the air that I expired pass into the opening, and the result was that the light went out because it lacked oxygen. My lungs took away the oxygen from the air, and there was no more to supply the combustion of the candle. It is, I think, very pretty to see the time it takes before the bad air that I throw into this part of the apparatus has reached the candle. The candle at first goes on burning, but as soon as the air from my lungs has had time to reach it, it goes out.

To consider this a little further, let us see what will happen with lime water. Here is a globe that contains a little lime water, and two pipes go through the stopper at the top [Fig. 25]. I can either draw in air (through A) and make the air that feeds my lungs go through the lime water, or I can force air out of my lungs (through B), which goes to the bottom, to show its effect upon the lime water.

However long I draw the **external air** into the lime water and then through it to my lungs, you

[Fig. 25] Two pipes go through a stopper into a globe, allowing air to be drawn in or out.

will observe that I shall produce no effect upon the water. It will not make the lime cloudy. But if I send the air from my lungs through the lime water several times in succession, you see how white and milky the water gets, showing the effect that **expired air** has had upon it. And now, you begin to understand that the atmosphere that we have spoiled by respiration is spoiled by carbon dioxide.

What is this process going on within us all day and night that we cannot do without? If we restrained our respiration, as we can to a certain extent, we would destroy ourselves. When we are asleep, the respiratory organs, and the parts that are associated with them, still go on with their necessary action. I must tell you, in the briefest possible manner, what this process is. We consume food, and that food goes through that strange set of vessels and organs within us. It is brought into various parts of the system, into the digestive parts especially. The air that we inhale and exhale is drawn into and thrown out of the lungs through a set of vessels so that the air and the food come close together, separated only by an exceedingly thin surface. The air can thus act upon the blood by this process, producing exactly the same kind of results we have seen in the case of the candle. The candle combines with parts of the air, forming carbon dioxide, and evolves heat, just as in the lungs there is this curious, wonderful change taking place. The entering oxygen combines with the carbon (not carbon in a free state, but, as in this case, in the right place and ready for action when required) and makes carbon dioxide, which is then thrown out into the atmosphere producing this unique result. Thus, we may look upon the food as fuel.

Look at this piece of sugar here. It is a compound of carbon, hydrogen, and oxygen, similar to a candle, although it contains the same elements in a different proportion, as shown in this table:

SUGAR

Carbon... 72
Hydrogen.................................... 11 } 99
Oxygen... 88

This is, indeed, a very curious thing, for the oxygen and hydrogen are in exactly the proportions that form water. Therefore, sugar may be said to be made up of 72 parts of carbon and 99 parts of water. And it is the carbon in the sugar that combines with the oxygen carried by the air in the process of respiration that makes us like candles. It produces these actions, warmth, and other far more wonderful results for the **sustenance** of the system. It is a beautiful and simple process. To make this still more striking, I will take some syrup, which contains about three-fourths sugar and a little water. If I put a little concentrated sulfuric acid in it, it takes away the water and leaves the carbon in a black mass. You see how the carbon is coming out, and before long, we shall have a solid mass of charcoal, all of which has come out of sugar. Sugar, as you know, is food, and here we have a solid mass of carbon where you would not have expected it.

Now, if I **oxidize** the carbon of sugar, we shall see a much more striking result. Here is some sugar, and here I have an **oxidizer**. This oxidizer is a quicker one than the atmosphere, and so we shall oxidize this fuel by a process similar to respiration but in a different form. It is the combustion of the carbon by the contact of oxygen that the substance has supplied to it. If I set this into action, you will see combustion produced. There it goes. Just what occurs in my lungs—taking in oxygen from another source, the atmosphere—takes place here by a more rapid process.

You will be astonished when I tell you what this curious play of carbon amounts to. A candle will burn some four, five, six, or seven hours. What, then, must be the daily amount of carbon going up into the air in the way of carbon dioxide! What a quantity of carbon must go from each of us in respiration! What a wonderful change of carbon must take place under these circumstances of combustion or respiration! A person in twenty-four hours converts as much as 200 grams of carbon into carbon dioxide. A dairy cow will convert 2,000 grams, and a horse around 2,200 grams, solely by the act of respiration. That is, the horse in twenty-four hours burns 2,200 grams of charcoal, or carbon, in its respiratory organs, to supply its natural warmth in that time. All the warm-blooded animals get their warmth in this way, by the conversion of carbon, not in a free state, but in a state of combination. And what an extraordinary view this gives us of the changes going on in our atmosphere. As much as 548 tons of carbon dioxide is formed by respiration in London alone in twenty-four hours. And where does all this go? Up into the air. How wonderful it is to find that the change produced by respiration, which seems so dangerous to us (for we cannot breathe the same air twice), is the very life and support of plants and vegetables that grow upon the surface of the earth. It is the same also under the surface, in the great bodies of water, for fishes and other animals **respire** upon the same principle.

Such fish as I have here respire using the oxygen that is dissolved from the air by the water, forming carbon dioxide. They all move about to produce a system whereby the animal and vegetable **kingdoms** rely on each other. And all the plants growing upon the surface of the earth, like these that I have here, absorb carbon. Their leaves take up their carbon from the atmosphere, to which we have given it in the form of carbon dioxide, and they grow and prosper. Give them a pure air like ours, and they could not live in it; give them carbon with other matter, and they live and rejoice. This plant, like all plants, gets its carbon from the atmosphere, which, as we have seen, carries away what is bad for us and, at the same time, good for them. So we are made dependent, all nature tied together by the laws that make one part help to bring about the good of another.

There is another little point that I must mention before we draw to a close, a point that concerns the whole of these operations. In this jar is some powdered **lead**. See what happens when I open the jar. You see how wonderfully combustible it is. The moment the air crept in, it acted. Now, there is a case of **chemical affinity** by which all our operations proceed. When we breathe, the same operation is going on within us. When we burn a candle, the attraction of the different parts, one to the other, is going on. Here it is going on in this case of the lead, and it is a beautiful instance of chemical affinity. If the products of combustion rose off from the surface, the lead would take fire and go on burning to the end. But you remember that we have this difference between charcoal and lead. While the lead can start into action at once if it has access to air, carbon will remain as it is for days, weeks, months, or years. The manuscripts of **Herculaneum** were written with carbonaceous ink, and there they have been for 1,800 years or more, not having been changed by the atmosphere at all, though coming in contact with it under various circumstances.

Now, what is the circumstance that makes the lead and carbon differ in this respect? It is a striking thing to see that the matter that is appointed to serve the purpose of fuel waits in its action. It does not start off burning, like the lead and many other things that I could show you, but it waits for action. This waiting is a curious and wonderful thing. Candles do not start into action at once like the lead, but there they wait for years, perhaps for ages, without undergoing any **alteration**.

Here I have a little gunpowder and some **guncotton**. Even these things differ in the conditions under which they will burn. The gunpowder is composed of carbon and other substances, making it highly combustible, and the guncotton is another combustible preparation. They are both waiting, but they will start into activity at different degrees of heat, or under different conditions. By applying a heated wire to them like this, we shall see which will start first. You see the guncotton has gone off, but not even the hottest part of the wire is now hot enough to fire the gunpowder. How beautifully that shows you the difference in the degree in which substances act in this way! In the one case, the substance will wait until the associated substances are made active by heat, but in the other, as in the process of respiration, it doesn't wait at all. In the lungs, as soon as the air enters, it unites with the carbon. Even in the lowest temperature that the body can bear short of being frozen, the action begins at once, producing the carbon dioxide of respiration. Thus, you see the analogy between respiration and combustion is rendered still more beautiful and striking.

All I can say to you at the end of these lectures (for all things come to an end sooner or later) is that I hope you will be worthy of being compared to a candle, and that, like a candle, you will shine as a light to those around you. I hope that in all your actions, you will do justice to the beauty of a candle by being honorable and successful in carrying out your duty to others.

Word List

A

□ **about** 熟 be about to まさに〜しようとしている，〜するところだ bring about 引き起こす fly about 飛び回る，飛び交う move about 動き回る

□ **absolutely** 副 完全に，確実に

□ **absorb** 動 吸収する

□ **abundance** 名 豊富，大量

□ **abundantly** 副 豊富に，おおいに

□ **access** 名 ①接近，近づく方法，通路 ②（システムなどへの）アクセス

□ **accompany** 動 ①ついていく，つきそう ②（〜に）ともなって起こる

□ **according** 副《 – to 〜》〜によれば[よると]

□ **accumulate** 動 ①蓄積する，積もる ②積み上げる，積み重ねる

□ **achieve** 動 成し遂げる，達成する，成功を収める

□ **acid** 形 ①酸っぱい ②酸性の 名 酸 muriatic acid 塩酸《塩化水素の水溶液。胃液の主成分》 sulfuric acid 硫酸《工業上もっとも重要な強酸の一つ》

□ **acidic** 形 酸っぱい，酸の

□ **act** 名 行為，行い 動 ①行動する ② 機能する ③演じる

□ **action** 熟 capillary action 毛細管現象《液体中に立てた毛管内の液面が，管外の液面より高く，または低くなる現象》 chemical action 化学作用 combined action 複合［総合］作用

□ **active** 形 ①活動的な ②積極的な ③活動［作動］中の

□ **activity** 名 活動，活気

□ **actually** 副 実際に，本当に，実は

□ **add** 動 ①加える，足す ②足し算をする ③言い添える

□ **additional** 形 追加の，さらなる

□ **adhere** 動《〜に》くっつく

□ **advantageous** 形 都合のよい，有利な

□ **affect** 動 影響する

□ **affinity** 名 密接な関係，類似性，親近感 chemical affinity 化学親和力《化合物をつくる際に元素間に働くと考えられる結びつきやすさ》

□ **after all** やはり，結局

□ **afterward** 副 その後，のちに

□ **ah** 間《驚き・悲しみ・賞賛などを表して》ああ，やっぱり

□ **air** 熟 air inlet 吸気口 expired air 呼気 open air 戸外，野外

□ **air-tight** 形 (容器などが) 空気を通さない, 気密の

□ **alcohol** 名 アルコール

□ **alike** 形 よく似ている

□ **alkali** 名 アルカリ《水に溶けて強い塩基性 (酸と結合して塩を生成する性質) を示す物質》

□ **all** 熟 after all やはり, 結局 all at once 一度にそろって, 突然, 出し抜けに all day and night 昼も夜もずっと, 24時間 all the way down 端から端まで, ずっと向こう [下ったところ] first of all まず第一に for all ~ ~にもかかわらず not ~ at all 少しも [全然] ~ない

□ **allow** 動 ①許す, 《- … to ~》が~するのを可能にする, …に~させておく ②与える

□ **along** 熟 go along ~に沿って行く

□ **alter** 動 (部分的に) 変える, 変わる

□ **alteration** 名 変更, 手直し

□ **although** 接 ~だけれども, ~にもかかわらず, たとえ~でも

□ **altogether** 副 まったく, 全然, 全部で 名 全体

□ **amount** 名 ①量, 額 ②《the - 》合計 動 (総計~に) なる amount to ~を意味する

□ **analogy** 名 ①類似 (点) ②類推

□ **analysis** 名 分析, 解析 (学)

□ **analyze** 動 分析する, 解析する, 細かく検討する

□ **and so** そこで, それだから, それで

□ **and yet** それなのに, それにもかかわらず

□ **animal and vegetable kigdom** 動植物界

□ **another** 熟 yet another さらにもう一つの

□ **antimony** 名 アンチモン《銀白色の金属光沢をもつ半金属元素。メッキ, 活字合金, 軸受合金, 半導体, 医薬品などに用いられる》

□ **antimony trisulfide** 三硫化アンチモン《灰色の光沢ある結晶性の塊状物質, あるいは灰黒色の粉末。濃塩酸と反応し硫化水素を発生する。輝安鉱として天然に産する。色ガラス, マッチ, 花火の製造に, また顔料として用いられる》

□ **any** 熟 in any way 決して, 多少なりとも not ~ any longer もはや~でない [~しない]

□ **anything else** ほかの何か

□ **apart** 副 ①ばらばらに, 離れて ②別にして, それだけで take apart 分解する

□ **apparatus** 名 装置, 器具

□ **apparent** 形 明らかな, 明白な, 見かけの, 外見上の

□ **apparently** 副 見たところ~らしい, 明らかに

□ **appear** 動 ①現れる, 見えてくる ②(~のように) 見える, ~らしい appear to するように見える

□ **appearance** 名 ①現れること, 出現 ②外見, 印象

□ **applicable** 形 適用できる, 応用できる

□ **application** 名 ①申し込み, 応募, 申し込み書 ②適用, 応用

□ **apply** 動 ①申し込む, 志願する ②あてはまる ③適用する

□ **appoint** 動 ①任命する, 指名する ②(日時・場所などを) 指定する be appointed to ~に任命される

□ **arrange** 動 ①並べる, 整える ②取り決める ③準備する, 手はずを整える

□ **arranged** 形 配置された

□ **arrangement** 名 ①準備, 手配 ②取り決め, 協定 ③整頓, 配置

□ **articulate** 形 (発音などが) はっきりした, 歯切れのよい

□ **as** 熟 as A so B Aと同様にB as far as ~と同じくらい遠く, ~ま

A
B
C
D
E
F
G
H
I
J
K
L
M
N
O
P
Q
R
S
T
U
V
W
X
Y
Z

で，～する限り（では）**as far as one can** できるだけ **as if** あたかも～のように，まるで～みたいに **as long as** ～する以上は，～である限りは **as much as** ～と同じだけ **as soon as** ～するとすぐ，～するや否や **as though** あたかも～のように，まるで～みたいに **as well as** ～と同様に **as you know** ご存知のとおり **as ～ as one can** できる限り **～ be known as** ～として知られている **just as** （ちょうど）であろうとおり **look upon ～ as** ～を…と見なす **see ～ as …** ～を…と考える **speak of ～ as** ～のことを…だと言う **such ～ as …** …のような～ **the same ～ as …** …と同じ（ような）～

□ **ascend** 動上がる，上る
□ **ascending** 形上昇する，上行性の
□ **ascending current** 上昇気流
□ **asleep** 形眠って（いる状態の）
□ **associate** 動連合[共同]する，提携する
□ **assume** 動①仮定する，当然のことと思う ②引き受ける
□ **astonished** 形びっくりした，驚いた
□ **at** 熟 **at first** 最初は，初めのうちは **at last** ついに，とうとう **at least** 少なくとも **at length** ついに，長々と，詳しく **at once** すぐに，同時に **at one time** ある時には，かつては **at the end of** ～の終わりに
□ **atmosphere** 名大気，空気
□ **atmospheric** 形大気の
□ **attempt** 動試みる，企てる
□ **attention** 名注意，集中
□ **attract** 動引きつける，引く
□ **attraction** 名引きつけるもの
□ **away** 熟 **carry away** 運び去る **come away** ～から離れて行く **go away** 立ち去る **melt away** 溶けてなくなる **run away** 走り去る，逃げ出す **take away** ①連れ去る ②取り上げる，奪い去る ③取り除く **throw**

away ～を捨てる

B

□ **bad-burning** 形燃え（方）が悪い
□ **badly** 副①悪く，まずく，へたに ②とても，ひどく
□ **balance** 名てんびん
□ **balanced** 形均衡を保っている，平衡状態の
□ **balloon** 名風船，気球
□ **barrel** 名たる **gun barrel** 銃身
□ **basic** 形基礎の，基本の **basic function** 基本機能
□ **basin** 名たらい，洗面器
□ **battery** 名電池，バッテリー
□ **bear** 動①運ぶ ②支える ③耐える
□ **beautifully** 副美しく，立派に，見事に
□ **beauty** 名①美，美しい人[物] ②《the –》美点
□ **because of** ～のために，～の理由で
□ **become of** ～はどうなるのか
□ **before long** やがて，まもなく
□ **beforehand** 副①あらかじめ，前もって ②早まって
□ **behave** 動振る舞う
□ **behind** 前①～の後ろに，～の背後に ②～に遅れて，～に劣って 副①後ろに，背後に ②遅れて，劣って **leave behind** あとにする，～を置き去りにする
□ **being** 動 be（～である）の現在分詞
□ **bell** 名ベル，鈴，鐘
□ **bell jar** 鐘形ガラス
□ **below** 前①～より下に ②～以下の，～より劣る 副下に[へ]
□ **beneath** 前～の下に[の]，～より低い 副下に，劣って

□ **bent** 形曲がった

□ **besides** 前①~に加えて，~のほかに ②《否定文・疑問文で》~を除いて

□ **best-looking** 形いちばんよく[魅力的に]見える

□ **better** 熟get better 良くなる，好転する had better ~したほうが身のためだ，~しなさい

□ **bit** 名①小片，少量 ②《a-》少し，ちょっと

□ **black-looking** 形黒く見える

□ **bladder** 名ぼうこう

□ **blast** 名突風，ひと吹き

□ **bleaching** 名漂白

□ **blocked** 形塞がれた，詰まった

□ **blood** 名血，血液

□ **blow** 動①(風が)吹く，(風が)~を吹き飛ばす ②息を吹く blow out 吹き消す

□ **blown** 動blow (吹く)の過去分詞

□ **board** 名板

□ **boil** 動沸騰する[させる]，煮える，煮る

□ **boiler** 名ボイラー，給湯器

□ **boiling** 形煮え立った，沸き立った

□ **both** 熟both A and BAもBも

□ **bottom** 名底，下部

□ **brass** 名真ちゅう(製品)《銅と亜鉛の合金》

□ **break out** 発生する，急に起こる，(戦争が)勃発する

□ **break up** ばらばらになる，解散させる

□ **breath** 名息，呼吸

□ **breathe** 動呼吸する

□ **brief** 形簡単な

□ **brightly** 副明るく，輝いて，快活に

□ **brightness** 名明るさ，輝き

□ **bring about** 引き起こす

□ **broaden** 動広がる，広げる

□ **bubble** 名泡

□ **burn out** 燃え尽きる

□ **burn with** ~を伴って燃える

□ **burner** 名バーナー，火口，ガス台

□ **burning** 形燃えている

□ **burst** 動①爆発する[させる] ②破裂する[させる]

□ **but** 熟not ~ but … ~ではなくて… nothing but ただ~だけ，~にすぎない，~のほかは何も…ない

□ **by far** 群を抜いて，間違いなく

□ **by means of** ~を用いて，~によって

□ **by nature** 生まれつき

□ **by virtue of** ~によって

C

□ **calcareous** 形石灰質の，炭酸カルシウムの

□ **calcium** 名カルシウム《単体は銀白色の軟らかい金属。酸や温水とは激しく反応して水素を発生する。天然には大理石・石灰岩・石膏などに含まれる。骨，歯などの主成分》

□ **calcium carbonate** 炭酸カルシウム《酸に溶けて二酸化炭素を発生し，二酸化炭素を含む水には炭酸水素カルシウムとなって溶ける。天然には方解石，石灰石，大理石などとして産出。セメント，顔料，歯みがき粉，医薬品などに使用される》

□ **calculate** 動①計算する，算出する ②見積もる，予想する

□ **can** 熟as far as one can できるだけ as ~ as one can できる限り~

□ **candle** 名ろうそく

□ **candlestick** 名ろうそく立て

□ **capillary** 形毛細管現象の

□ **capillary action** 毛細管現象《液

99

体中に立てた毛管内の液面が, 管外の
液面より高く, または低くなる現象》

□ **carbon** 图炭素《炭素族元素の一つ。
無定形炭素・黒鉛・ダイヤモンドの三
つの同素体が存在するが, 化合物とし
ては岩石圏, 水圏, 大気圏, 生物圏な
どに非常に豊富に存在する。きわめて
融解しにくく, 高温では昇華する》

□ **carbon dioxide** 二酸化炭素, 炭
酸ガス《炭素とその化合物の完全燃焼,
生物の呼吸や発酵の際などに生じる
気体。無色, 無臭, 不燃性の気体で空
気より重い》

□ **carbonaceous** 图炭素(質)の
carbonaceous series 炭素質系の物
質

□ **carbonate** 图炭酸塩《炭酸の水素
原子が金属で置換されて生じる塩》
calcium carbonate 炭酸カルシウム
《酸に溶けて二酸化炭素を発生し, 二
酸化炭素を含む水には炭酸水素カル
シウムとなって溶ける。天然には方
解石, 石灰石, 大理石などとして産出。
セメント, 顔料, 歯みがき粉, 医薬品
などに使用される》

□ **carry away** 運び去る

□ **carry forward** 前進させる

□ **carry out** [計画を]実行する

□ **case** 熟 **in the case of** ～の場合は

□ **cast** 動(影を)投げかける **cast a
shadow on** ～の上に影を落とす 图
鋳造(物)

□ **cast iron** 鋳鉄

□ **certain** 图①ある ②いくらかの

□ **chalk** 图白墨, チョーク

□ **channel** 图通路, 水路, 経路

□ **character** 图特性, 個性

□ **charcoal** 图木炭

□ **charring** 图焦げ目, 黒焼け

□ **chemical** 图化学の, 化学的な
chemical action 化学作用
chemical affinity 化学親和力《化合
物をつくる際に元素間に働くと考え
られる結びつきやすさ》

□ **chemically** 圃化学的に(見て)

□ **chemist** 图化学者

□ **chemistry** 图化学, 化学的性質,
化学反応

□ **chimney** 图煙突(状のもの)

□ **chlorate** 图塩素酸塩《塩素酸の水
素が金属元素で置換されて生じる塩》
potassium chlorate 塩素酸カリウ
ム《熱すると酸素を放って分解する
ので酸化剤に用いられる。硫黄, リン,
有機物などと混ぜると加熱, 衝撃など
によって爆発。マッチ, 花火など爆薬
の原料, 漂白剤, 医薬品の製造に用い
られる》

□ **circumstance** 图(周囲の)事情,
状況, 環境

□ **clap** 動(手を)たたく

□ **clear** 图はっきりした, 明白な

□ **clearly** 圃明らかに, はっきりと

□ **climate** 图気候, 風土, 環境

□ **closed** 图閉じた, 閉鎖した

□ **closely** 圃①密接に ②念入りに,
詳しく ③ぴったりと

□ **coal** 图石炭, 木炭

□ **collapse** 動崩壊する, 崩れる

□ **colorless** 图無色の

□ **column** 图(円)柱

□ **combination** 图結合(状態, 行
為)

□ **combine** 動結合する[させる]

□ **combined** 图結び付いた, 化合し
た **combined action** 複合[総合]作
用

□ **combust** 動燃える, (～を)燃や
す

□ **combustible** 图可燃の, 可燃[燃
焼]性の

□ **combustion** 图燃焼 **imperfect
combustion** 不完全燃焼

□ **come away** ～から離れて行く

□ **come in contact with** ～と接
触する

□ **come out** 出てくる, 姿を現す
come out of ～から出てくる

□ **come over** やって来る

□ **compare** 動 比較する, 対照する
be compared to ～と比較して, ～
に比べれば

□ **comparison** 名 比較, 対照

□ **completely** 副 完全に, すっかり

□ **complicated** 形 複雑な

□ **compose** 動 構成する,《be -d of
～》～から成り立つ

□ **composition** 名 組織, 組成, 構成

□ **compound** 形 合成の, 複合の 名
合成物, 化合物, 複合物

□ **compressibility** 名 圧縮性

□ **concentrated** 形 凝縮された, 高
濃度の, 濃厚な

□ **concern** 動 関係する

□ **concerning** 前 ～についての, 関
しての

□ **conclusion** 名 結論, 結末

□ **condensable** 形 (液体などが) 凝
縮 [濃縮] できる

□ **condensation** 名 凝縮, 濃縮

□ **condense** 動 濃縮する

□ **condensed** 形 凝縮 [濃縮] された

□ **condensing** 名 凝縮, 濃縮 形 凝
縮 [濃縮] させる

□ **condition** 名 ① (健康) 状態, 境遇
②《-s》状況, 様子 ③条件

□ **conduct** 動 ①指導する ②実施す
る, 処理 [処置] する

□ **confine** 動 制限する, 閉じ込める

□ **confined** 形 閉じ込められた, 限ら
れた

□ **conical** 形 円すい形の

□ **connected** 形 結合した, 関係のあ
る

□ **consider** 動 ①考慮する, ～しよう
と思う ②(～と) みなす ③気にかけ
る, 思いやる

□ **consist** 動《- of ～》(部分・要素
から) 成る

□ **consume** 動 ①消費する, 費やす
②消滅させる ③摂取する

□ **contact** 熟 come in contact with
～と接触する

□ **contain** 動 含む, 入っている

□ **content** 名《-s》中身, 内容

□ **continuous** 形 連続的な, 継続す
る, 絶え間ない

□ **contract** 動 縮小する

□ **control** 名 ①管理, 支配 (力) ②抑
制 go out of control 制御不能にな
る

□ **conversion** 名 転換, 変換, 転向

□ **convert** 動 変える, 転換する, 改宗
させる

□ **convey** 動 ①運ぶ ②伝達する, 伝
える ③譲渡する

□ **convince** 動 納得させる, 確信さ
せる

□ **cool down** 冷ます, 涼しくする

□ **copper** 形 銅の, 銅製の

□ **coral** 名 サンゴ (珊瑚)

□ **cork** 名 コルク, コルク栓 [製品]

□ **cotton** 名 ①綿, 綿花 ②綿織物, 綿
糸

□ **could** 熟 Could you ～? ～して
くださいますか。 How could ～?
何だって～なんてことがありえよう
か?

□ **couple** 名 ①2つ, 対 ②数個 a
couple of 2, 3の

□ **course** 熟 of course もちろん, 当
然

□ **cover** 動 覆う, 包む 名 覆い, カバ
ー

□ **cow** 名 雌牛, 乳牛 dairy cow 乳牛

□ **crack** 名 割れ目, ひび

□ **creep** 動 ゆっくり動く

□ **crept** 動 creep (ゆっくり動く) の

過去, 過去分詞

□ **cubic** 形 立方体の

□ **cubic foot** 立方フィート（ft³）
《1 ft³ = 1,728 in³ = 28,317 cm³》

□ **cubic inch** 立方インチ（in³）
《1 in³ = 16.36 cm³》

□ **curious** 形 好奇心の強い, 珍しい,
奇妙な, 知りたがる

□ **curiously** 副 ①不思議なことに
②もの珍しそうに

□ **current** 名 流れ, 電流 ascending
current 上昇気流

□ **cylinder** 名 ①円柱, 円筒 ②シリ
ンダー

D

□ **daily** 形 毎日の, 日常の

□ **dairy** 形 牛乳の, 酪農の dairy cow
乳牛

□ **damp** 形 湿っぽい, じめじめした

□ **darkish** 形 黒ずんだ

□ **day** all day and night 昼も夜も
ずっと, 24時間 day and night 昼も
夜も the other day 先日

□ **deal** 動《– with ～》～を扱う 名（不
特定の）量, 額 a good [great] deal
(of ～) かなり［ずいぶん・大量］(の
～), 多額（の～）

□ **deceive** 動 だます, あざむく

□ **decompose** 動 ①腐敗する, 腐敗
させる ②分解する

□ **decrease** 動 減少する

□ **degree** 名（温度・角度の）度

□ **deliver** 動 配達する, 伝える

□ **dense** 形 濃い, 密集した

□ **depend** 動《– on [upon] ～》①～
を頼る, ～をあてにする ②～による

□ **dependent** 形 頼っている, ～次
第である

□ **describe** 動（言葉で）描写する, 特
色を述べる, 説明する

□ **destroy** 動 破壊する, 絶滅させる,
無効にする

□ **determine** 動 ①決心する［させ
る］②決定する［させる］③測定する

□ **diagram** 名 図表, 図式, 図解

□ **differ** 動 異なる, 違う, 意見が合わ
ない

□ **different from**《be –》～と違う

□ **differently** 副（～と）異なって,
違って

□ **digestive** 形 消化の, 消化を助け
る

□ **diluted** 形（液体が）薄められた,
希釈された

□ **dim** 形 薄暗い, 見にくい

□ **dimness** 名 薄暗さ, 不明瞭

□ **dioxide** 名 二酸化物《酸素2原子が
他の元素と結合した化合物》carbon
dioxide 二酸化炭素, 炭酸ガス《炭素
とその化合物の完全燃焼, 生物の呼吸
や発酵の際などに生じる気体。無色,
無臭, 不燃性の気体で空気より重い》

□ **direction** 名 方向, 方角

□ **directly** 副 ①じかに ②まっすぐ
に ③ちょうど

□ **dirt** 名 汚れ, 泥, ごみ

□ **dirty** 形 汚い, 汚れた

□ **disappear** 動 見えなくなる, 姿を
消す, なくなる

□ **disappointed** 形 がっかりした,
失望した

□ **discuss** 動 議論［検討］する

□ **dissolve** 動 溶ける, 溶かす

□ **distance** 名 距離, 隔たり, 遠方

□ **distant** 形 遠い, 隔たった, 距離の
ある

□ **distinct** 形 ①独特な ②はっきり
した

□ **distinguish** 動 ①見分ける, 区別
する ②特色づける ③相違を見分け

る

□ **disturbance** 图乱すこと, 妨害 (物), じゃま

□ **disturbed** 形かき乱された, 動揺した, 不安な

□ **double** 形①2倍の, 二重の ②対の

□ **down** 熟 all the way down 端から端まで, ずっと向こう [下ったところ] の cool down 冷ます, 涼しくする fall down 落ちる go down 下に降りる pass down (次の世代に) 伝える run down (液体が) 流れ落ちる, 駆け下りる turn ~ upside down ~を上下逆さまにする upside down 逆さまに

□ **downward** 副下方へ, 下向きに, 堕落して, ~以後

□ **draw** 動引く, 引っ張る draw in 吸い込む, 引き込む draw off (水などを) 抜く, 流し出す. draw out 引き出す draw to a close 終わりに近づく draw up 引き上げる

□ **drawing** 图素描

□ **drawn** 動 draw (引く) の過去分詞

□ **drive out** 追い出す drive ~ out of …から~を追い出す

□ **driven** 動 drive (車で行く) の過去分詞

□ **due** 形 due to ~によって, ~が原因で

□ **duty** 图①義務 (感), 責任 ②職務, 任務

□ **dye** 图染料

E

□ **each other** お互いに

□ **earth** 熟 in the earth 地中に

□ **easily** 副①容易に, たやすく, 苦もなく ②気楽に

□ **edge** 图端, 縁

□ **effect** 图影響, 効果, 結果

□ **either A or B** Aかそれともに B

□ **elasticity** 图弾力性, 弾性, 伸縮性

□ **electric** 形電気の, 電動の

□ **electrolysis** 图電気分解, 電解《電解質水溶液あるいは溶融塩などのイオン伝導体に, 電流を流して化学変化をおこさせること》

□ **element** 图要素, 成分, 元素

□ **elementary** 形①初歩の ②単純な, 簡単な

□ **elementary substance** 単体

□ **else** 熟 anything else ほかの何か or else さもないと

□ **elsewhere** 副どこかほかの所で [へ]

□ **end** 熟 at the end of ~の終わりに

□ **energetic** 形エネルギッシュな, 精力的な, 活動的な

□ **enough to do** ~するのに十分な

□ **enter into** ~に入る

□ **entire** 形全体の, 完全な, まったくの

□ **entirely** 副完全に, まったく

□ **equally** 副等しく, 平等に

□ **escape** 動逃げる, 免れる, もれる

□ **essential** 形本質的な, 必須の

□ **even if** たとえ~でも

□ **everything** 代すべてのこと [もの], 何でも, 何もかも

□ **everywhere** 副どこにいても, いたるところに

□ **evidently** 副明白に, 明らかに

□ **evolve** 動進化する [させる], 発展する [させる]

□ **examine** 動試験する, 調査 [検査] する, 診察する

□ **exceedingly** 副はなはだしく, 非常に

□ **except** 前~を除いて, ~のほかは except for ~を除いて, ~がなけれ

ば

- □ **excess** 名 ①超過, 過剰 ②不節制 **in excess** 過度に
- □ **exhale** 動 息を吐く
- □ **exhaust** 動 排出する
- □ **exhibit** 動 展示する, 見せる, 示す
- □ **exist** 動 存在する, 生存する, ある, いる
- □ **existence** 名 存在, 実在, 生存
- □ **expand** 動 ①広げる, 拡張[拡大] する ②発展させる, 拡充する
- □ **expansibility** 名 伸張性, 膨張性
- □ **expansion** 名 拡大, 拡張, 展開
- □ **expect** 動 予期[予測]する, (当然 のこととして)期待する
- □ **experiment** 名 実験, 試み
- □ **expire** 動 息を吐く
- □ **expired** 形 (息が)吐き出された
- □ **expired air** 呼気
- □ **explanation** 名 説明, 解説, 釈明
- □ **explode** 動 爆発する[させる]
- □ **exploration** 名 探検, 実地調査
- □ **explosion** 名 爆発, 急増
- □ **extent** 名 範囲, 程度, 広さ, 広がり
- □ **exterior** 名 外側, 外見, 外観
- □ **external** 形 外部の, 外側の
- □ **external air** 外気
- □ **extinguish** 名 (火などを)消す
- □ **extraordinary** 形 異常な, 並はず れた, 驚くべき
- □ **extremely** 副 非常に, 極度に

F

- □ **fact** 熟 **in fact** つまり, 実は, 要するに
- □ **fail** 動 失敗する
- □ **fall down** 落ちる

- □ **fall into** 流れ込む
- □ **fallen** 動 fall (落ちる)の過去分詞
- □ **far** 熟 **as far as** 〜と同じくらい遠く, 〜まで, 〜する限り(では) **as far as one can** できるだけ **by far** 群を抜いて, 間違いなく
- □ **fasten** 動 固定する, 結ぶ, 締まる
- □ **fault** 名 ①欠点, 短所 ②過失, 誤り
- □ **feed** 動 ①食物を与える ②供給する
- □ **filings** 名 やすり粉[くず] **iron filings** 鉄粉
- □ **filled with** 《be –》〜でいっぱいになる
- □ **find out** 見つけ出す, 知る, 解明する
- □ **fire** 熟 **set fire** 火をつける **set fire to** 〜に火を付ける
- □ **fireplace** 名 暖炉
- □ **firmly** 副 しっかりと, 断固として
- □ **first** 熟 **at first** 最初は, 初めのうちは **first of all** まず第一に
- □ **fit** 動 (形や大きさが)合う, 適合する
- □ **fixed** 形 固定した, ゆるぎない
- □ **flame** 名 炎, (炎のような)輝き
- □ **flask** 名 フラスコ
- □ **flat** 形 平らな
- □ **float** 動 浮く, 浮かぶ
- □ **flow** 動 流れ出る, 流れる
- □ **fluid** 名 流動体 形 流体の, 流動的な
- □ **fly about** 飛び回る, 飛び交う
- □ **fly off** 飛び去る
- □ **focus** 動 ①焦点を合わせる ②(関心・注意を)集中させる
- □ **focused** 形 集中的な
- □ **following** 形 《the –》次の, 次に続く
- □ **foot** 名 フィート《長さの単位。約 30.48cm》 **cubic foot** 立方フィート

（ft³）《1 ft³ = 1,728 in³ = 28,317 cm³》

□ **for all ～** ～にもかかわらず

□ **for instance** たとえば

□ **for oneself** 独力で, 自分のために

□ **for years** 何年も for ～ years ～ 年間, ～年にわたって

□ **force** 图力, 勢い 動①強制する, 力ずくで～する, 余儀なく～させる ②押しやる, 押し込む

□ **form** 图形, 形式 動形づくる

□ **former** 形前の, 先の, 以前の

□ **forward** 副①前方に ②先へ, 進 んで carry forward 前進させる

□ **free** 熟set free (人)を解放する, 釈 放される, 自由の身になる

□ **freely** 副自由に, 障害なしに

□ **freeze** 動凍る, 凍らせる

□ **frequently** 副頻繁に, しばしば

□ **frozen** 動freeze (凍る)の過去分詞 形凍った

□ **fuel** 图燃料

□ **full of**《be－》～で一杯である

□ **fully** 副十分に, 完全に, まるまる

□ **fume** 图(有害な)煙, 蒸気, ガス

□ **function** 图機能, 作用 basic function 基本機能

□ **furnace** 图炉, かまど, 溶鉱炉, 厳 しい試練

□ **furnish** 動供給する

□ **further** 形いっそう遠い, その上の, なおいっそうの 副いっそう遠く, そ の上に, もっと

G

□ **g** 略グラム (gram)

□ **gain** 動①得る, 増す ②進歩する, 進む

□ **gas** 图ガス, 気体

□ **gaseous** 形ガス (状)の, 気体の

□ **gauze** 图ガーゼ

□ **general** 形全体の, 一般の, 普通の

□ **generate** 動生み出す, 引き起こ す

□ **generator** 图発電機, 発生器

□ **get better** 良くなる, 好転する

□ **get hold of** ～を手に入れる, ～ をつかむ

□ **get in** 中に入る

□ **get out of** ～から外へ出る[抜け 出る]

□ **get to** ～に達する[到着する]

□ **give out** 放つ, 放出する

□ **give rise to** ～を生じさせる

□ **globe** 图球, 球体

□ **glorious** 形荘厳な, すばらしい

□ **glow** 動(火が)白熱して輝く

□ **go** 熟go along ～に沿って行く go away 立ち去る go down 下に降り る go home 帰宅する go in 中に入 る go into ～に入る go off①去る, なくなる, 消える ②生じる ③爆発 する go on 続く, 続ける, 進み続け る, 起こる, 発生する go out①(火・ 明かりが)消える ②外へ出る go out of control 制御不能になる go through 通り抜ける go up ～に上 がる, 登る

□ **good-looking** 形姿・形の良い

□ **govern** 動治める, 管理する, 支配 する

□ **gradually** 副だんだんと

□ **gram** 图グラム《重さの単位》

□ **grate** 图①炉の火格子 ②(窓の) 格子

□ **gravity** 图重力, 引力

□ **great deal of**《a－》多量の, 大量 の

□ **groove** 图溝, わだち

□ **gun** 图銃, 大砲 gun barrel 銃身

□ **guncotton** 图綿火薬《火薬類に用

105

いられるニトロセルロース。精製した綿花を硫酸と硝酸で処理して作る。無煙火薬とダイナマイトの原料となる》

□ **gunpowder** 名黒色火薬《硝石, 木炭, 硫黄の粉末を混ぜた火薬。火薬の中で最も古くから用いられ, 今日では花火や口火などに使用》

□ **gutter** 名溶けたろうそくのろうの流出

□ **guttering** 名ろうそくの溶けたろうが流れること

H

□ **had better** ～したほうが身のためだ, ～しなさい

□ **halves** 名half (半分) の複数

□ **hang** 動かかる, かける, つるす, ぶら下がる

□ **happen to** たまたま～する, 偶然～する

□ **healthily** 副健康で

□ **heat** 名熱

□ **heated** 形熱せられた, 熱くなった

□ **heaviness** 名重いこと, 重さ

□ **height** 名高さ

□ **hemisphere** 名半球 (体)

□ **Herculaneum** 名ヘルクラネウム《イタリア南部, ベスビオ火山西麓にあった古代都市。紀元後79年のベスビオ火山の噴火により熱泥流に襲われ, ポンペイとともに埋没した》

□ **here is** こちらは～です。

□ **highly** 副①大いに, 非常に ②高度に, 高位に ③高く評価して, 高価で

□ **hold** 熟get hold of ～を手に入れる, ～をつかむ

□ **hollow** 形うつろな, くぼんだ

□ **home** 熟go home 帰宅する

□ **honorable** 形①尊敬すべき, 立派な ②名誉ある ③高貴な

□ **horizontal** 形地平線の, 水平線の, 水平の

□ **hot** 熟red hot (金属などが) 赤熱した

□ **how** 熟How could ～? 何だって～なんてことがありえようか? no matter how どんなに～であろうとも

□ **however** 副たとえ～でも however long どんなに長く 接けれども, だが

□ **hydrogen** 名水素

I

□ **if** 熟as if あたかも～のように, まるで～みたいに even if たとえ～でも

□ **ignite** 動火がつく [つける], 発火する

□ **ignition** 名発火, 点火

□ **illumination** 名照明

□ **illustration** 名説明

□ **imagine** 動想像する, 心に思い描く

□ **immediately** 副すぐに, ～するやいなや

□ **imperfect** 形不完全な, 未完成な

□ **imperfect combustion** 不完全燃焼

□ **imperfection** 名①不完全, 不十分 ②欠陥, 欠点

□ **in** 熟in fact つまり, 実は, 要するに in order to ～するために, ～しようと in place of ～の代わりに in the case of ～の場合は in the earth 地中に in the meantime それまでは, 当分は in the middle of ～の真ん中 [中ほど] in this way このようにして in time やがて

□ **inactive** 形不活性な

□ **incandescent** 形白熱する, 光り輝く

- [ ] **inch** 名 インチ《長さの単位。1/12 フィート，2.54cm》 **cubic inch** 立方インチ（in^3）《$1\ in^3 = 16.36\ cm^3$》 **square inch** 平方インチ（in^2）《$1\ in^2 = 6.45\ cm^2$》
- [ ] **include** 動 含む，勘定に入れる
- [ ] **incondensable** 形 凝縮できない，濃縮できない
- [ ] **increase** 動 増加［増強］する，増やす，増える
- [ ] **indeed** 副 ①実際，本当に ②《強意》まったく
- [ ] **independence** 名 独立心，自立
- [ ] **independent** 形 独立した，自立した
- [ ] **indifferent** 形 （反応に対して）中性の
- [ ] **individual** 形 独立した，個性的な，個々の
- [ ] **inhale** 動 吸い込む，吸入する
- [ ] **ink** 名 インク
- [ ] **inlet** 名 注入口，吸気口 **air inlet** 吸気口
- [ ] **instance** 名 ①例 ②場合，事実 **for instance** たとえば
- [ ] **instantly** 副 すぐに，即座に
- [ ] **instead** 副 その代わりに
- [ ] **instrument** 名 道具，器具，器械
- [ ] **intense** 形 強烈な，激しい
- [ ] **interesting** 形 おもしろい，興味を起こさせる
- [ ] **interfere** 動 じゃまをする，干渉する
- [ ] **inverted** 形 （上下が）逆さまの，反転した
- [ ] **invisible** 形 目に見えない
- [ ] **iron** 名 鉄，鉄製のもの **cast iron** 鋳鉄 形 鉄の，鉄製の
- [ ] **iron filings** 鉄粉
- [ ] **irregular** 形 不規則な，ふぞろいの
- [ ] **irregularity** 名 不規則，ふぞろい，不規則な事（物）
- [ ] **irregularly** 副 不規則に，ふぞろいに
- [ ] **issue** 動 （～から）出る，生じる
- [ ] **itself** 代 それ自体，それ自身

J

- [ ] **jar** 名 （広口の）瓶，壺 **bell jar** 鐘形ガラス
- [ ] **judge** 動 判断する，評価する
- [ ] **just as** （ちょうど）であろうとおり
- [ ] **justice** 名 公平，公正，正当，正義

K

- [ ] **keep out** （場所に）入らせない，締め出す，～を外に出したままにする
- [ ] **kind of** ある程度，いくらか，～のようなもの［人］
- [ ] **kingdom** 名 王国，～界 **animal and vegetable kingdom** 動植物界
- [ ] **know** 熟 **as you know** ご存知のとおり **you know** ご存知のとおり，そうでしょう
- [ ] **known as** 《be –》～として知られている

L

- [ ] **lack** 動 不足している，欠けている 名 不足，欠乏
- [ ] **lamp** 名 ランプ，灯火 **oil lamp** 石油ランプ
- [ ] **largely** 副 大いに，主として
- [ ] **last** 熟 **at last** ついに，とうとう
- [ ] **later** 熟 **sooner or later** 遅かれ早かれ
- [ ] **lead** 名 鉛《青白色の軟らかくて重い金属。加工が容易。空気中では表面が

酸化されて被膜となるが、内部に及ばない。鉛管・電線被覆材・はんだ・活字合金・蓄電池極板・放射線遮蔽材などに使用される》

- □ **least** 名最小, 最少 at least 少なくとも
- □ **leave behind** あとにする, 〜を置き去りにする
- □ **lecture** 名講義
- □ **length** 名長さ at length ついに, 長々と, 詳しく
- □ **less** 形〜より小さい[少ない] 副〜より少なく, 〜ほどでなく
- □ **let in** 〜を招き入れる
- □ **let us** どうか私たちに〜させてください
- □ **lift** 動持ち上げる, 上がる
- □ **lighted** 形火のついている
- □ **like** 熟 like this このような, こんなふうに look like 〜のように見える, 〜に似ている would like to 〜したいと思う
- □ **lime** 名石灰《生石灰(酸化カルシウム), または, 消石灰(水酸化カルシウム)のこと》
- □ **limestone** 名石灰岩[石]《炭酸カルシウムを主成分とする堆積岩。海底に堆積した生物の遺骸が堆積した生物岩と, 化学的沈殿による化学岩とがある。建築用材や石灰, セメントの原料など広く用いられる》
- □ **limit** 名限界
- □ **liquid** 名液体 形液体(状)の, 流動する
- □ **lit** 動 light (火をつける)の過去, 過去分詞
- □ **liter** 名リットル, リッター
- □ **living** 形生きている
- □ **locomotive** 名機関車
- □ **London** 名ロンドン《英国の首都》
- □ **long** 熟 as long as 〜する以上は, 〜である限りは before long やがて, まもなく however long どんなに長

く

- □ **longer** 熟 no longer もはや〜でない[〜しない] not 〜 any longer もはや〜でない[〜しない]
- □ **look** 熟 look like 〜のように見える, 〜に似ている look upon 〜 as 〜を…と見なす take a look at 〜をちょっと見る
- □ **lower** 動下げる, 低くする
- □ **luminous** 形光輝く
- □ **lung** 名肺
- □ **lycopodium** 名石松子《ヒカゲノカズラ(ヒカゲノカズラ科の常緑性シダ)の胞子から作った粉末。花粉増量剤として使われる》

M

- □ **made of** 《be – 》〜でできて[作られて]いる
- □ **made to** 《be – 》〜させられる
- □ **made up of** 《be – 》〜で構成されている
- □ **make up** 作り出す, 〜を構成[形成]する
- □ **make 〜 into** 〜を…にする
- □ **manganese** 名マンガン《純粋な単体は銀白色。空気中では表面が酸化される。希酸に溶けて水素を発生させる。鉄鋼業において脱酸, 脱硫剤, また合金の構成金属として広く用いられている》
- □ **manganese oxide** 酸化マンガン《黒褐色の粉末である二酸化マンガンは, 高温に熱すると分解し酸素を発生する。酸化剤, 染料, 釉, マッチ, 乾電池, マンガン鋼の材料として利用される》
- □ **manner** 名方法, やり方
- □ **manuscript** 名原稿, 手書き原稿, 写本
- □ **marble** 名大理石

108

- [ ] **mass** 图①固まり, (密集した)集まり ②質量
- [ ] **material** 图材料, 原料
- [ ] **matter** 熟a matter of ～の問題 no matter how どんなに～であろうとも not matter 問題にならない
- [ ] **means** 熟by means of ～を用いて, ～によって
- [ ] **meantime** 图合間, その間 in the meantime それでは, 当分は
- [ ] **measure** 图①寸法, 測定, 計量, 単位 ②程度, 基準
- [ ] **medical** 形医学の
- [ ] **melt** 動①溶ける, 溶かす ②(感情が)和らぐ, 次第に消え去る melt away 溶けてなくなる
- [ ] **mention** 動(～について)述べる, 言及する
- [ ] **merely** 副単に, たかが～に過ぎない
- [ ] **metallic** 形金属の, 金属性の
- [ ] **method** 图方法, 手段
- [ ] **middle** 图中間, 最中 in the middle of ～の真ん中[中ほど]に
- [ ] **might** 助《mayの過去》①～かもしれない ②～してもよい, ～できる
- [ ] **milky** 形乳のような, 乳白色の
- [ ] **mineral** 图鉱物, 鉱石
- [ ] **mix** 動①混ざる, 混ぜる ②(～を)一緒にする mix in 混入する, よく混ぜ合わせる
- [ ] **mixture** 图①混合 ②入り混じったもの
- [ ] **moderate** 形穏やかな, 適度な
- [ ] **moisture** 图水分, 湿気, 湿度
- [ ] **moment** 图①瞬間, ちょっとの間 ②(特定の)時, 時期
- [ ] **more** 熟more and more ますます more of ～よりももっと more than ～以上 no more もう～ない
- [ ] **moss** 图コケ《植物》
- [ ] **move about** 動き回る

- [ ] **much** 熟as much as ～と同じだけ too much 過度の
- [ ] **multitude** 图多数, 大勢
- [ ] **muriatic** 形塩酸の
- [ ] **muriatic acid** 塩酸《塩化水素の水溶液。胃液の主成分》

N

- [ ] **namely** 副すなわち, つまり
- [ ] **nasty** 形不快な
- [ ] **naturally** 副生まれつき, 自然に, 当然
- [ ] **nature** 熟by nature 生まれつき
- [ ] **nearly** 副①近くに, 親しく ②ほとんど, あやうく
- [ ] **necessary** 形必要な, 必然の
- [ ] **need to do** ～する必要がある
- [ ] **neither** 代(2者のうち)どちらも～でない 副《否定文に続いて》～も…しない neither ～ nor … ～も…もない
- [ ] **next time** 次回に
- [ ] **nicely** 副①うまく, よく ②上手に, 親切に, 几帳面に
- [ ] **nicely-adjusted** 形うまく調整された
- [ ] **night** 熟all day and night 昼も夜もずっと, 24時間 day and night 昼も夜も
- [ ] **nitrogen** 图窒素《単体は無色・無味・無臭の気体。空気中に体積で約78パーセント含まれる。室温では不活性で燃焼に関与しない。高温では多くの元素と直接反応する》
- [ ] **no longer** もはや～でない[～しない]
- [ ] **no matter how** どんなに～であろうとも
- [ ] **no more** もう～ない
- [ ] **noise** 图騒音, 騒ぎ, 物音

A B C D E F G H I J K L M N O P Q R S T U V W X Y Z

□ **none** 代 (~の)何も[誰も・少しも] …ない

□ **nor** 接 ~もまたない **neither ~ nor … ~**も…もない

□ **not matter** 問題にならない

□ **not yet** まだ~してない

□ **not ~ any longer** もはや~でない[~しない]

□ **not ~ at all** 少しも[全然]~ない

□ **not ~ but …** ~ではなくて…

□ **nothing but** ただ~だけ、~にすぎない、~のほかは何も…ない

□ **notice** 動 気づく、認める

□ **now that** 今や~だから、~からには

O

□ **object** 名 ①物、事物 ②目的物、対象

□ **oblong** 名 長方形、楕円形

□ **observe** 動 ①観察[観測]する、監視[注視]する ②気づく

□ **obtain** 動 得る、獲得する

□ **occupy** 動 ①占領する、保有する ②占める

□ **occur** 動 (事が)起こる、生じる

□ **occurrence** 名 発生、出来事

□ **of course** もちろん、当然

□ **of which** ~の中で

□ **oil** 名 油、石油 **oil lamp** 石油ランプ

□ **once** 熟 **all at once** 一度にそろって、突然、出し抜けに **at once** すぐに、同時に

□ **one** 熟 **at one time** ある時には、かつては **one of ~**の1つ[人] **one side** 片側

□ **oneself** 熟 **for oneself** 独力で、自分のために

□ **onto** 前 ~の上へ[に]

□ **opaque** 形 不透明な、くすんだ

□ **open air** 戸外、野外

□ **opening** 名 開いた所、穴

□ **operation** 名 操作、作業、動作

□ **opportunity** 名 好機、適当な時期[状況]

□ **or else** さもないと

□ **order** 熟 **in order to ~**するために、~しようと

□ **ordinary** 形 普通の、通常の

□ **organ** 名 (体の)器官 **respiratory organ** 呼吸器官

□ **other** 熟 **each other** お互いに **the other day** 先日

□ **ought** 動 《– to ~》当然~すべきである、きっと~するはずである

□ **our test gas** 一酸化二窒素 (nitrous oxide)のこと《亜酸化窒素、笑気ガスとも言い、それ自体は無色の気体だが、酸素に触れると化合して褐色の二酸化窒素(nitrogen dioxide)となる》

□ **out** 熟 **break out** 発生する、急に起こる、(戦争が)勃発する **burn out** 燃え尽きる **carry out** [計画を]実行する **come out** 出てくる、姿を現す **come out of ~**から出てくる **draw out** 引き出す **drive out** 追い出す **drive ~ out of …**から~を追い出す **find out** 見つけ出す、知る、解明する **get out of ~**から外へ出る[抜け出る] **give out** 放つ、放出する **go out** ①(火・明かりが)消える ②外へ出る **go out of control** 制御不能になる **keep out** (場所に)入らせない、締め出す、~を外に出したままにする **out of** ①~から外へ、~から抜け出して ②~から作り出して、~を材料として ③~の範囲外に、~から離れて **point out** 指し示す、指摘する **pour out** ~に注ぎだす **put out** (明かり・火を)消す **send out** 使いに出す、派遣する、発送する **take out** 取り除く、抜き取る **take ~ out of …**から~を得る[奪う] **throw out** 放り出す

□ **over** 塾 come over やって来る
run over 一走りする，〜の上を走る

□ **oxide** 名酸化物《酸素と他の元素と
の化合物》manganese oxide 酸化
マンガン《黒褐色の粉末である二酸化
マンガンは，高温に熱すると分解し酸
素を発生する。酸化剤，染料，釉，マッ
チ，乾電池，マンガン鋼の材料として
利用される》

□ **oxidize** 動酸化させる

□ **oxidizer** 名酸化剤《酸化作用をも
つ物質。酸素を与える物質，水素をう
ばう物質，電子を受け取る物質をいう。
過マンガン酸カリウムなど》

□ **oxygen** 名酸素

P

□ **pale** 形 (色が)薄い，(光が)薄暗い

□ **palm** 名手のひら(状のもの)

□ **particle** 名粒子，小さな粒

□ **particular** 形固有の，特有の，特
別な

□ **partly** 副一部分は，ある程度は

□ **pass down** (次の世代に)伝える

□ **pass through** 〜を通る，通行す
る

□ **pass up into** 〜の中に入り込ん
でしまう

□ **passage** 名通過，通行，通路

□ **perfection** 名完全，完成

□ **perfectly** 副完全に，申し分なく

□ **perform** 動(任務などを)行う，果
たす，実行する

□ **perhaps** 副たぶん，ことによると

□ **permanent** 形永続する，永久の，
長持ちする

□ **phenomena** 名 phenomenon (現
象)の複数

□ **phenomenon** 名現象，事象

□ **philosopher** 名哲学者，賢者

□ **philosopher's candle** 賢者の
ともし火《ガラス管を通したコルク栓
でフタをした薬ビンの中に亜鉛の小
片とうすい酸 (希硫酸など) を入れた
もの。化学変化により水素が発生し，
管の先から噴き出すので点火すると
弱い炎をあげて燃える》

□ **phosphorus** 名リン《非金属元素
の一つ。黄リン(白リン)・紫リン・黒
リンなどの同素体がある。黄リンは蝋
状の固体で毒性が強く，空気中に置く
と自然発火する》

□ **photograph** 名写真

□ **pile** 名①積み重ね，(〜の)山 ②電
池 voltaic pile ボルタ電池《1800年
ごろにイタリアのボルタによって発
明された，希硫酸の溶液に，銅を正極，
亜鉛を負極として入れた電池》動積
み重ねる，積もる pile up 積み重ね
る

□ **pillar** 名柱，支柱

□ **pint** 名パイント《単位；英国で約
0.568リットル》

□ **pipe** 名管，筒，パイプ

□ **place** 塾 in place of 〜の代わりに
take place 行われる，起こる

□ **plate** 名(浅い) 皿

□ **platinum** 名白金，プラチナ《銀白
色の貴金属。化学的にはきわめて安定
で王水以外の酸に不溶。酸化・還元の
触媒するつぼ・電極・理化学用器械・
装飾品などに用いる》形プラチナ製
[色]の

□ **plenty** 名十分，たくさん，豊富
plenty of たくさんの〜

□ **point out** 指し示す，指摘する

□ **pole** 名電極

□ **poorly** 副①貧しく，乏しく ②へ
たに

□ **popgun** 名豆鉄砲

□ **porous** 形多孔質の

□ **portion** 名一部，分け前

□ **position** 名位置，場所，姿勢

□ **positive** 形 ①正の, 陽の ②確かな・疑いようがない

□ **possible** 形 ①可能な ②ありうる, 起こりうる

□ **potassium** 名 カリウム《軟らかい銀白色の金属。化学的には非常に活性で, 水, 酸素, 酸と激しく反応する。水と反応すると水素を発生し, 水酸化カリウムを生成する》

□ **potassium chlorate** 塩素酸カリウム《熱すると酸素を放って分解するので酸化剤に用いられる。硫黄, リン, 有機物などと混ぜると加熱, 衝撃などによって爆発。マッチ, 花火など爆薬の原料, 漂白剤, 医薬品の製造に用いられる》

□ **pound** 名 ポンド《重量の単位。453.6g》 動 どんどんたたく, 打ち砕く

□ **pounded** 形 砕いた

□ **pour** 動 ①注ぐ, 浴びせる ②流れ出る, 流れ込む **pour out** ～に注ぎだす

□ **powder** 名 粉末

□ **powdered** 形 粉になった, 粉末の

□ **powerfully** 副 強力に, 強烈に

□ **preparation** 名 準備, したく

□ **presence** 名 存在すること

□ **preserve** 動 保存[保護]する, 保つ

□ **press** 動 圧する, 押す, プレスする

□ **pressure** 名 プレッシャー, 圧力, 圧縮, 重荷

□ **prevent** 動 ①妨げる, じゃまする ②予防する, 守る, 《－ from …》～が…できない[しない]ようにする

□ **previously** 副 あらかじめ, 以前に[は]

□ **principle** 名 原理, 原則

□ **proceed** 動 進む, 進展する, 続ける

□ **process** 名 過程, 経過, 進行

□ **product** 名 産物

□ **production** 名 製造, 生産

□ **proof** 名 証拠, 証明

□ **proper** 形 適切な

□ **properly** 副 適切に, きっちりと

□ **property** 名 性質, 属性

□ **proportion** 名 割合, 比率

□ **propose** 動 申し込む, 提案する

□ **prosper** 動 栄える, 繁栄する, 成功する

□ **prove** 動 ①証明する ②(～である ことが) わかる, (～と) なる

□ **pull up** 引っ張り上げる

□ **pump** 名 ポンプ 動 ポンプで汲む

□ **pure** 形 純粋な, 混じりけのない

□ **put in** ～の中に入れる

□ **put on** ～を…の上に置く

□ **put out** (明かり・火を) 消す

□ **put over** ～の上に置く, (火) に掛ける

□ **put ～ into …** ～を…の状態にする, ～を…に突っ込む

□ **pyrotechnic** 名 花火

Q

□ **quality** 名 質, 性質, 品質

□ **quantity** 名 量

□ **quickly** 副 敏速に, 急いで

R

□ **raise** 動 ①上げる, 高める ②起こす

□ **rapid** 形 速い, 急な, すばやい

□ **rapidly** 副 速く, 急速 すばやく, 迅速に

□ **rather** 副 ①むしろ, かえって ②かなり, いくぶん, やや ③それどころか逆に **rather than** ～よりむしろ

WORD LIST

- ☐ **rattle** 動 がたがたいう, がたがた音を立てる
- ☐ **reasoning** 名 推論
- ☐ **recall** 動 思い出す, 思い出させる
- ☐ **recognize** 動 認める, 認識[承認]する
- ☐ **red heat** 赤熱温度
- ☐ **red hot** (金属などが)赤熱した
- ☐ **red-colored** 形 赤色の
- ☐ **redden** 動 赤くなる[する]
- ☐ **reduce** 動 ①減じる ②しいて～させる, (～の)状態にする
- ☐ **re-enter** 動 再び入る
- ☐ **reference** 名 言及, 参照, 照会 with reference to ～に関連して
- ☐ **regard** 名 as regards ～に関しては with regard to ～に関しては
- ☐ **regular** 形 ①規則的な, 秩序のある ②定期的な, 一定の, 習慣的
- ☐ **rejoice** 動 喜ぶ
- ☐ **relate** 動 関連がある, かかわる, うまく折り合う
- ☐ **relationship** 名 関係, 関連, 血縁関係
- ☐ **release** 動 解き放す, 釈放する
- ☐ **relight** 動 再び火がつく
- ☐ **relit** 動 relight (再び火がつく)の過去, 過去分詞
- ☐ **rely** 動 (人が…に)頼る, 当てにする
- ☐ **remain** 動 ①残っている, 残る ②(～の)ままである[いる]
- ☐ **remark** 名 注意, 注目, 観察
- ☐ **remarkable** 形 ①異常な, 例外的な ②注目に値する, すばらしい
- ☐ **render** 動 (～を…に)する, 表す
- ☐ **represent** 動 ①表現する ②意味する ③代表する
- ☐ **require** 動 必要とする, 要する
- ☐ **research** 名 調査, 研究

- ☐ **resist** 動 抵抗[反抗・反撃]する, 耐える
- ☐ **resistance** 名 抵抗《加えられた力に対して, それと反対の方向にはたらく力。特に, 物体や流水の運動をさまたげ, エネルギーの損失を伴う現象》
- ☐ **respect** 名 (特定の)点, 事項
- ☐ **respiration** 名 呼吸(作用)
- ☐ **respiratory** 形 呼吸の
- ☐ **respiratory organ** 呼吸器官
- ☐ **respire** 動 呼吸する
- ☐ **restrain** 動 ①(人・動物の行動を)制する, 抑制する ②こらえる ③拘束する
- ☐ **result** 名 結果
- ☐ **resume** 動 再び始める, 再開する
- ☐ **retain** 動 ①保つ, 持ち続ける ②覚えている
- ☐ **return to** ～に戻る, ～に帰る
- ☐ **ring** 名 輪, 円形, 指輪
- ☐ **ring-shaped** 形 リング状の, 輪状の
- ☐ **rise** 熟 give rise to ～を生じさせる
- ☐ **rising** 形 昇る, 高まる
- ☐ **roughly** 副 おおよそ, 概略的に, 大ざっぱに
- ☐ **rubber** 名 ゴム, 消しゴム
- ☐ **run away** 走り去る, 逃げ出す
- ☐ **run down** (液体が)流れ落ちる, 駆け下りる
- ☐ **run over** 一走りする, ～の上を走る
- ☐ **rush** 動 突進する, せき立てる

S

- ☐ **safely** 副 安全に, 間違いなく
- ☐ **same** 熟 the same ～ as …と同じ(ような)～
- ☐ **saturated** 形 飽和した

113

A
B
C
D
E
F
G
H
I
J
K
L
M
N
O
P
Q
R
S
T
U
V
W
X
Y
Z

☐ **saturated solution** 飽和溶液《一定温度のもとで溶解しうる最大の溶質を溶かした溶液》

☐ **scale** 图規模, 割合, 程度, スケール

☐ **see** 熟 see ～ as … ～を…と考える you see あのね, いいですか

☐ **seem** 動 (～に)見える, (～のように)思われる

☐ **send out** 使いに出す, 派遣する, 発送する

☐ **separate** 動 分ける, 分かれる, 隔てる 形 分かれた, 別々の

☐ **separately** 副 離れて, 独立して, 別々に

☐ **separation** 图 分離(点), 離脱, 分類, 別離

☐ **series** 图 シリーズ, ひとそろい, セット carbonaceous series 炭素質系の物質

☐ **serve** 動 ①仕える, 奉仕する ②(役目を)果たす, 務める, 役に立つ

☐ **set fire** 火をつける set fire to ～ に火を付ける

☐ **set free** (人)を解放する, 釈放される, 自由の身になる

☐ **shadow** 图 影, 暗がり cast a shadow on ～の上に影を落とす throw a shadow 影を落とす

☐ **shake** 動 振る, 揺れる, 揺さぶる

☐ **shape** 图 形, 姿, 型

☐ **shell** 图 貝がら

☐ **shine** 動 光る, 輝く

☐ **short of** ～に達していない, ～の手前で

☐ **show someone in** [人を]中に案内する, 招き入れる

☐ **shown** 動 show (見せる)の過去分詞

☐ **shut** 動 ①閉まる, 閉める, 閉じる ②たたむ ③閉じ込める ④shutの過去, 過去分詞

☐ **side** 图 側, 横, そば, 斜面 one side 片側

☐ **significance** 图 重要(性), 意味, 深刻さ

☐ **significantly** 副 有意に, 著しく, かなり

☐ **similar** 形 同じような, 類似した, 相似の

☐ **similarly** 副 同様に, 類似して, 同じように

☐ **simply** 副 ①簡単に ②単に, ただ ③まったく, 完全に

☐ **sink** 動 沈む, 沈める

☐ **slide** 動 滑る, 滑らせる

☐ **slight** 形 わずかな

☐ **smoke** 動 煙を出す 图 煙, 煙状のもの

☐ **so** 熟 and so そこで, それだから, それで as A so B Aと同様にB so that ～するために, それで, ～できるように so ～ that … 非常に～なので…

☐ **soap** 图 石けん soap suds 石けんの泡

☐ **sole** 形 唯一の, 単独の

☐ **solely** 副 1人で, 単独で, 単に

☐ **solid** 形 固体[固形]の

☐ **solid mass** 固体塊

☐ **solid substance** 固体

☐ **solution** 图 溶液, 溶体, 液剤 saturated solution 飽和溶液《一定温度のもとで溶解しうる最大の溶質を溶かした溶液》

☐ **something** 代 ある物, 何か

☐ **somewhat** 副 いくらか, やや, 多少

☐ **soon** 熟 as soon as ～するとすぐ, ～するや否や

☐ **sooner or later** 遅かれ早かれ

☐ **soot** 图 すす

☐ **sort** 图 種類, 品質 a sort of ～のようなもの, 一種の～

- □ **source** 名源, 原因, もと
- □ **speak of** ～を口にする **speak of ～ as** ～のことを…だと言う
- □ **splinter** 名 (木・竹などの) 細片
- □ **spoil** 動台なしにする, だめになる
- □ **sponge** 名スポンジ, 海綿
- □ **square** 名平方の
- □ **square inch** 平方インチ (in²)《1 in² = 6.45 cm²》
- □ **start off** ～し始める
- □ **state** 名あり様, 状態 動述べる, 表明する
- □ **stay in** (場所に) とどまる, 維持する
- □ **steady** 形 ①しっかりした, 安定した, 落ち着いた ②堅実な, まじめな
- □ **steam** 名蒸気, 湯気
- □ **stick** 動 ①(突き) 刺さる, 刺す ②くっつく, くっつける ③突き出る **stick up** 上に突き出る
- □ **stopcock** 名 (水道管などの) 栓
- □ **stopper** 名 ①栓, 詰め, 止め具 ②止める人, ストッパー
- □ **strangely** 副奇妙に, 変に, 不思議なことに, 不慣れに
- □ **stream** 名流れ 動流れ出る, 流れる
- □ **strength** 名強度, 濃度
- □ **stretch** 動引き伸ばす, 広がる, 広げる
- □ **striking** 形著しい, 目立つ
- □ **structure** 名構造, 骨組み, 仕組み
- □ **stuff** 動詰める, 詰め込む
- □ **subsequent** 形次の, 続いて起きる, その結果生じた
- □ **substance** 名 ①物質, 物 ②実質, 中身, 内容 **elementary substance** 単体 **solid substance** 固体
- □ **succeed** 動 ①成功する ②(～の) 跡を継ぐ
- □ **successful** 形成功した, うまくいった

- □ **succession** 名連続, 相続, 継承 **in succession** 連続して
- □ **such a** そのような
- □ **such ～ as ...** …のような～
- □ **such ～ that ...** 非常に～なので…
- □ **suction** 名吸引, 吸引力
- □ **suction cup** 吸着カップ
- □ **suds** 名石けん水, 石けんの泡 **soap suds** 石けんの泡
- □ **sufficient** 形十分な, 足りる
- □ **sufficiently** 副十分に, 足りて
- □ **suitability** 名適合 (性)
- □ **sulfuric** 形硫黄の
- □ **sulfuric acid** 硫酸《工業上もっとも重要な強酸の一つ》
- □ **supply** 動供給 [配給] する, 補充する 名供給 (品), 給与, 補充
- □ **support** 動 ①支える, 支持する ②養う, 援助する
- □ **supporting** 形支える, 支持する
- □ **suppose** 動 ①仮定する, 推測する ②《be -d to ～》～することになっている, ～するものである
- □ **surface** 名表面
- □ **surround** 動囲む, 包囲する
- □ **surrounding** 形周囲の
- □ **suspend** 動ぶらさがる, つるす, 一時停止する, 延期する
- □ **sustain** 動持ちこたえる, 持続する, 維持する, 養う
- □ **sustenance** 名 (生命の) 維持, 食物, 生計
- □ **syrup** 名シロップ

T

- □ **take** 熟 **take a look at** ～をちょっと見る **take apart** 分解する **take**

☐ **away** ①連れ去る ②取り上げる, 奪い去る ③取り除く **take from** 〜から引く, 選ぶ **take in** 取り入れる, 取り込む **take out** 取り除く, 抜き取る **take place** 行われる, 起こる **take up** 取り上げる, 拾い上げる **take 〜 out of** …から〜を得る[奪う]

☐ **taper** 名細長い小ろうそく, 先端に行くほど細くなるろうそく

☐ **taste** 名味

☐ **temperature** 名温度, 体温

☐ **than** 熟 **more than** 〜以上 **rather than** 〜よりむしろ

☐ **that** 熟 **now that** 今や〜だから, 〜からには **so that** 〜するために, それで, 〜できるように **so 〜 that …** 非常に〜なので… **such 〜 that …** 非常に〜なので…

☐ **therefore** 副 したがって, それゆえ, その結果

☐ **thick** 形 ①厚い ②(測った幅が)〜の厚さの

☐ **thin** 形 薄い, 細い

☐ **this** 熟 **in this way** このようにして **like this** このような, こんなふうに

☐ **thoroughly** 副 すっかり, 徹底的に

☐ **though** 副 しかし **as though** あたかも〜のように, まるで〜みたいに

☐ **three-fourths** 名 4分の3

☐ **through** 熟 **go through** 通り抜ける **pass through** 〜を通る, 通行する

☐ **throw a shadow** 影を落とす

☐ **throw away** 〜を捨てる

☐ **throw off** (匂い・煙・熱・光を)発する, 放つ

☐ **throw out** 放り出す

☐ **throw up** 跳ね上げる

☐ **thrown** 動 throw (投げる)の過去分詞

☐ **thunderstorm** 名 (激しい)雷雨

☐ **thus** 副 ①このように ②これだけ ③かくて, だから

☐ **tight** 形 堅い, きつい, ぴんと張った 副 堅く, しっかりと

☐ **tightly** 副 きつく, しっかり, 堅く

☐ **time** 熟 **at one time** ある時には, かつては **in time** やがて **next time** 次回に

☐ **tin** 名 錫(すず), ブリキ

☐ **tobacco** 名 たばこ

☐ **ton** 名 トン《重量・容積単位》

☐ **tongue** 名 舌

☐ **too much** 過度の

☐ **too 〜 to …** …するには〜すぎる

☐ **towel** 名 タオル

☐ **trace** 動 たどる, さかのぼって調べる

☐ **train of** 一連の, ひとつながりの

☐ **transfer** 動 ①移動する ②移す

☐ **transparent** 形 透明な, 透けて見える

☐ **transport** 動 輸送[運送]する

☐ **trisulfide** 名 三硫化物《複数の硫黄原子が直接結合した構造を持つ多硫化物の一つ。硫化物とは, 硫黄とそれよりも陽性の元素との化合物。多くは酸により分解して硫化水素を発生する》**antimony trisulfide** 三硫化アンチモン《灰色の光沢ある結晶性の塊状物質, あるいは灰黒色の粉末。濃塩酸と反応し硫化水素を発生。輝安鉱として天然に産する。色ガラス, マッチ, 花火の製造に, また顔料として用いられる》

☐ **truth** 名 真理, 事実

☐ **tube** 名 管, 筒

☐ **turn to** 〜の方を向く, 〜に変わる

☐ **turn up** (音量などを)上げる, 大きくする

☐ **turn 〜 upside down** 〜を上下逆さまにする

☐ **turpentine** 名 テレビン(精)油《松

やにから得られる揮発性の精油。無色
ないし淡黄色で特異臭のある液体。溶
剤・ワニス・ペイントなどの製造、油
絵の材料などに使用》

□ **two-thirds** 名3分の2

U

□ **unable** 形《be‐to～》～すること
ができない

□ **unchangeable** 形変わらない

□ **undergo** 動経験する、被る、耐え
る

□ **underneath** 前～の下に、～真下
に

□ **understanding** 名理解、意見の
一致、了解

□ **undissolved** 形溶解されていな
い

□ **uneven** 形平らでない、でこぼこの、
むらのある

□ **uninteresting** 形つまらない、退
屈な

□ **unique** 形唯一の、ユニークな、独
自の

□ **unite** 動①1つにする[なる]、合わ
せる、結ぶ ②結束する、団結する

□ **unlike** 前～と違って

□ **up** 熟be made up of ～で構成さ
れている break up ばらばらになる、
解散させる draw up 引き上げる go
up ～に上がる、登る make up 作り
出す、～を構成[形成]する pile up
積み重ねる pull up 引っ張り上げる
stick up 上に突き出る take up 取
り上げる、拾い上げる throw up 跳
ね上げる turn up (音量などを)上げ
る、大きくする up to ～まで、～に至
るまで、～に匹敵して warm up 暖
まる、温める

□ **upon** 前①《場所・接触》～(の
上)に ②《日・時》～に ③《関係・従
事》～に関して、～について、～して
depend upon ～に頼る look upon

～ as ～を…と見なす

□ **upper** 形上の、上位の、北方の

□ **upside** 名上側、上部 turn ～
upside down ～を上下逆さまにす
る upside down 逆さまに

□ **upward** 副上の方へ、上向きに

□ **upwards** 副上の方へ、上向きに

□ **us** 熟let us どうか私たちに～させ
てください

V

□ **vacuum** 名真空

□ **valve** 名弁、バルブ

□ **vapor** 名①蒸気、湯気 ②気体

□ **vaporize** 動(～を)蒸発させる

□ **vaporous** 形蒸気のような、蒸気
質の

□ **variety** 名①変化、多様性、寄せ集
め ②種類

□ **various** 形変化に富んだ、さまざ
まの、たくさんの

□ **vary** 動変わる、変える、変更する、
異なる

□ **vegetable** 名野菜、青物 形野菜の、
植物(性)の animal and vegetable
kingdom 動植物界

□ **very well** とても[大変・非常に]
よく

□ **vessel** 名①器、容器 ②管、脈管

□ **vial** 名(薬・香水などを入れる)小
瓶

□ **violent** 形暴力的な、激しい

□ **virtue** 名by virtue of ～によって

□ **visible** 形目に見える、明らかな

□ **volcanic** 形①火山の ②強烈な

□ **voltaic** 形(化学作用による)電流の

□ **voltaic pile** ボルタ電池《1800年
ごろにイタリアのボルタによって発
明された、希硫酸の溶液に、銅を正極、

亜鉛を負極として入れた電池》

□ **volume** 名①《-s》たくさん, 多量 ②量, 体積

W

□ **wait for** ～を待つ

□ **waiting** 名待機

□ **warm up** 暖める, 温める

□ **warm-blooded** 形 (動物が) 温血の

□ **warmth** 名暖かさ, 思いやり

□ **watch glass** 時計皿《液体の試料を載せて蒸発させたり, 蒸発を防ぐための覆いとして使ったりする, 実験用の丸い透明なガラスの皿》

□ **wax** 名ろう, ワックス

□ **way** 名the way down 端から端まで, ずっと向こう[下ったところ]の in any way 決して, 多少なりとも in this way このようにして way of ～する方法 way to ～する方法

□ **weigh** 動①(重さを)はかる ②重さが～ある

□ **weight** 名重さ, 重力, 体重

□ **well** 熟as well as ～と同様に very well とても[大変・非常に]よく

□ **wet** 形ぬれた, 湿った, 雨の

□ **whatever** 形①どんな～でも ②《否定文・疑問文で》少しの～も, 何らかの

□ **whenever** 接①～するときはいつでも, ～するたびに ②いつ～しても

□ **whereby** 副①～するところの, それによって ②どういう手段で, 何について

□ **whether** 接～かどうか, ～かまたは…, ～であろうとなかろうと

□ **which** 熟of which ～の中で

□ **whole** 形全体の, すべての, 完全な,

満～, 丸～ 名《the－》全体, 全部

□ **wick** 名 (ろうそくなどの) 芯

□ **width** 名幅, 広さ

□ **wipe** 動～をふく, ぬぐう, ふきとる

□ **wire** 名針金

□ **with** 熟be filled with ～でいっぱいになる burn with ～を伴って燃える come in contact with ～と接触する with reference to ～に関連して with regard to ～に関しては

□ **within** 副①～の中[内]に, ～の内部に ②～以内で, ～を越えないで

□ **without** 熟do without ～なしですませる

□ **wonder** 動①不思議に思う, (～に)驚く ②(～かしらと)思う

□ **wonderfully** 副不思議なほど, すばらしく

□ **worth** 形 (～の) 価値がある, (～)しがいがある

□ **worthy** 形価値のある, 立派な

□ **would like to** ～したいと思う

Y

□ **years** 熟for years 何年も for ～ years ～年間, ～年にわたって

□ **yet** 熟and yet それなのに, それにもかかわらず not yet まだ～してない yet another さらにもう一つの

□ **you** 熟Could you ～? ～してくださいますか。 as you know ご存知のとおり you know ご存知のとおり, そうでしょう you see あのね, いいですか

□ **yourselves** 代yourself (あなた自身) の複数

Z

□ **zinc** 图 亜鉛《青みをおびた銀白色の
金属。硫酸などの酸と反応して水素を
発生する。トタン板など鉄鋼製品のめ
っき, 乾電池の負極, 真ちゅうや洋銀
などの合金に使われる》

English Conversational Ability Test
国際英会話能力検定

● E-CATとは…
英語が話せるようになるための
テストです。インターネット
ベースで、30分であなたの発
話力をチェックします。

| www.ecatexam.com |

● iTEP®とは…
世界各国の企業、政府機関、アメリカの大学
300校以上が、英語能力判定テストとして採用。
オンラインによる90分のテストで文法、リー
ディング、リスニング、ライティング、スピー
キングの5技能をスコア化。iTEP®は、留学、就
職、海外赴任などに必要な、世界に通用する英
語力を総合的に評価する画期的なテストです。

| www.itepexamjapan.com |

ラダーシリーズ
The Chemical History of a Candle ロウソクの科学

2023年1月9日　第1刷発行

原著者　マイケル・ファラデー

リライト　アンドリュー・ロビンス

発行者　浦　晋亮

発行所　**IBCパブリッシング株式会社**
〒162-0804 東京都新宿区中里町29番3号
菱秀神楽坂ビル
Tel. 03-3513-4511　Fax. 03-3513-4512
www.ibcpub.co.jp

© IBC Publishing, Inc. 2023

印　　刷　株式会社シナノパブリッシングプレス
装　　丁　伊藤 理恵
カバー写真　Photographed by 4028mdk09

Printed in Japan
ISBN978-4-7946-0743-0